LINCOLN E.C. GREENIDGE

NO MORE EXCUSES

Taking the first step to living a life of Purpose with Meaning

CONTENTS

FOREWORD

I strongly recommend reading this book *No More Excuses* by Lincoln E.C. Greenidge.

Lincoln has poured his heart, knowledge, and wisdom to share what he has learned from his parents and his life's experiences, to help you live your life with No More Excuses. The book has practical tips that are easy to follow, which will help you live the life that you deserve to reach your full potential regardless of your age, education, or financial situation; to do what you love and love what you do without excuses.

I was fortunate to get to know Lincoln and his family as their Natural Doctor to see him applying what he has written in his book to live his wellness journey without any excuses.

Regardless of your age, education, and knowledge, once you start reading this book, you will not be able to stop until you read the whole book, like I did. This book should be included in every school/college curriculum to teach students, during school and after graduation, to live their lives without excuses. The author referenced the following prayer, which he stated was one of the most powerful prayers one should embrace:

"God grant me the serenity to accept the things I cannot change, courage to change the things I can, and the wisdom to know the difference, living one day at a time;

enjoying one moment at a time; taking this world as it is and not as I would have it; trusting that You will make all things right if I surrender to Your will; so that I may be reasonably happy in this life and supremely happy with You forever in the next. Amen."
Reinhold Niebuhr

My desire is that all readers of this book reach Total Wellness (Physically, Mentally, and Spiritually), with No More Excuses.

Professor Dr. George Grant, Ph.D., M.Sc., M.Ed., B.SC. HONS., R.M., C.M., CBS

PREFACE

Somehow, growing up as a middle child with one sister almost a year older than me and my younger sister being seven years younger, I found myself always being sure of myself. Often, I thought it had nothing to do with me being an only boy or "my parents' influence on me. I know many would try to look for a connection, but I can tell you that there was none, at least none that could be easily seen, or so I thought.

However, as I got older, it became apparent that one could likely draw a parallel to my dad being very innovative and unafraid to try anything. He was a local preacher, a choir member, a senator (twice), a businessman, a union leader, a philanthropist, a humanitarian; basically, a man who lived life the way life should be led—a life of purpose with meaning.

I guess there was a connection, after all, as to why I never felt the need to conform or to believe I could not do anything if I wanted to achieve it.

Even though I often knew I could, I did not feel the urge to do much more than I felt. One could say that living a life of being average was comfortable, even though my mind thought otherwise, but overshadowed by an unwillingness to be in the light, thus remaining in the shadows. Having the desire to do many things at some point requires one to prioritize, even if at the very superficial level of understanding, and at many times making the mistake of prioritizing oneself into doing what is comfortable and not what is meaningful.

As a child, I never put much thought into living a life of purpose, as my parents, like many others, were programmed to direct their children to live a life of simplicity. I am not saying that simplicity is a bad thing, but given the unlimited potential that we all have in the power of our minds, why should we let it go to waste? It is not that our parents consciously thought of mediocrity as a level to attain, but their very actions, like many parents, seem to aspire to that level, likely in their very subconscious, through many years of programming from their parents and their parents' parents. My parents supported us tremendously in everything we did. They pushed us to pursue a higher level of education when it would have been acceptable to just continue working in the same job until retirement without any post-secondary education. What they did not do was bring us up to be 'leaders', but instead to be decent law-abiding citizens and contribute to the growth of our nation in whatever capacity we found ourselves. In short, to be morally upright and do our best. I am not sure what that means, but surely there is no manifestation of greatness and living a life of purpose with meaning, in what I call such shallow, average, and undefined aspirations.

No wonder many are likened to sheep as we conform and follow blindly, whether it be for safety or just because we lack the courage to believe in ourselves and our limitless potential. Consider the fact that the notion of children being masterpieces was foreign to our parents, as they, too, were taught to just work hard, never question authority, find a vocation, have a family, and teach their children to do the same; a repetitive act through the ages.

Never was it ever included that the power of the mind was indeed the greatest masterpiece ever created and that we all had such a mind to do amazing things. Imagine if all children were brought up to believe that they all had talents that needed to be found, nurtured, and harnessed to live a life of purpose in service to others.

What a world it would be. Some believe that our purpose on earth is to serve God. However, what does this really mean?

What if one does not believe in God? Are they doomed? Absolutely not! You see, many do not realize that whether you believe in God or not, your purpose is one of service to others, which can only be realized by using your talents to live such a life and by doing. The key word is "doing," as having faith without works (action) is futile. In fact, by this very notion, service to others is service to God—for those that truly believe. Again, it does not matter what or who you believe in if you do not ACT in a way that demonstrates a life of living to serve others in a meaningful way. Even the Pharisees spoke eloquently about the Law of Moses, but their actions were nowhere close to being in service to others as they sought everyone to serve them, given their self-imposed authority.

After my dad passed away from Colon Cancer, I had many questions, one of which was why God would allow someone like my dad to die at such a young age of 70. Especially given that my dad was a man who gave of himself and lived a life of purpose in the service of others. It took me a few years to realize that God did no such thing. Many want to blame God, someone, or something for life's tragedies and successes, but that is not valid in any way and hence the reason why excuses continue to be poison to the soul.

Regarding my dad's death, it was not God who caused his seemingly untimely demise, but it was just my dad's time to move on from this world into the next. Even though his physical body is no more, his spirit lives on, since he left a legacy for many to follow. What legacy? you may ask.

Well, it dawned on me that when we all pass this earth, what account would we give to show HOW we lived our life? Would we give excuses as to why we did not live a life of purpose with meaning? What legacy would we leave, or would we leave a legacy at all?

I also noticed the deterioration of the quality of service in most industries, which led me to think of why that would be the case. Then it hit me that fear and doubt permeated almost everyone's mind, which was not helped by the fact that most were programmed to never see the possibilities and potential within themselves, but instead conform to stereotypes and generational tendencies, indoctrinations, and superstitions. In addition, it would appear that many were being taught to be the victim and never the victor, so it invariably manifested in their work ethic and how they provided service to others.

Another observation I had is that many legitimized their behavior and had all the excuses in the world as to why they were not living a meaningful life and the life they would love to live. After all, life is not fair, so they should be given a pass. However, the fact that life is not fair does not mean that one should go through life with no joy and purpose.

I wrote this book to confront some of the many excuses that people use to not live a life of purpose with meaning. Ideally, the book exposes that ALL excuses, with no exceptions, are just that—excuses, as they have no validity and are driven by one's mind through insecurity, fear, and doubt. None of us, if asked whether our excuses are valid, can successfully support a response other than no, unless we make up other excuses for our excuses. Why is that? Well, the way I see it is that many of us are fearful of failing, of not conforming, or being on the outside. If we look in the mirror and ask ourselves the hard questions, we are always left with a feeling that we really do not have any excuses and that all our excuses result from fear and doubt that cripple us in every way.

When we look at anyone who has succeeded exceedingly, they all have failed in some way at least once, they have been on the outside, and none of them have conformed to norms and the limitations that society puts on critical thinking, innovation, and embracing the potential from within. So why should we seek to conform when there is nothing cool about being ordinary? The power from within us all calls us to be extraordinary and live a life without excuses, and one in the service of others, thus fulfilling our purpose with meaning.

I hope that at the end of the book, you will believe in yourself sufficiently to realize that your greatest satisfaction and success will come from service of others, by using your talents to live such a life with meaning, and to once and for all do away with the constant excuses that seem to be commonplace in our daily lives. Say yes to embracing the power from within; say yes to embracing your talents; say yes to going boldly to use such talents in the service of others; and for the last time, say "NO MORE EXCUSES!!!"

DEDICATION

This book of anecdotes has been completed with thanks and admiration to my father: the funniest, kindest, and most God-fearing man I have ever known. My Dad passed away in 2014, and he is the only individual I have been directly acquainted with who lived a life of purpose. He was kind to everyone and unapologetic in his deeds of service to others without wanting, expecting, or requesting anything in return. Though his life experience saw him being a Senator (twice), a union leader, a humanitarian, an entrepreneur, a television evangelist, and a lay preacher, he was more spiritual than religious, demonstrating his purpose in his deeds and not just his words. He lived what he preached; he was what he preached. I will be forever grateful for his legacy and the example he set for me and everyone else to follow. Naturally, I will never be my father, but I thank God that my dad left a legacy for myself and others to be ourselves and fulfill the same purpose with the skills, gifts, and talents with which we have been blessed.

It would be remiss of me not to share one of the many stories that encapsulate the kind of man my father was.

One day after arriving home from school, I entered my room and, for some reason, my eye captured the fact that a pair of my shoes was missing. I did not have many shoes, and it was apparent that the space between my church shoes and house shoes was empty. I first wondered whether I had somehow misplaced them but realized it was not possible, so I called out to my dad, who was in the other room, and asked whether he had seen the shoes.

He came into my room with his normal smile and pleasant demeanor and said, "I noticed that you had not worn these shoes for some time now, and on my way home, I saw a man walking down the road who had no shoes. Remembering that you did not need the shoes and thinking they might fit the man, I rushed home, then returned to the man and gave them to him." What does a son say to such an act of kindness? There were many more similar acts, but I thought I would share this one. Many would be upset, but I did not have the heart to be so selfish. I could write this entire book on my experiences with my dad, but it would take away from the intent of this book.

To My Mother

I give thanks to my mother for being the rock of the family. They say it takes a village to bring up a child, and I can say she has been the cornerstone of that village in many ways. While my dad pursued helping everyone he met, my mother supported him in all his activities and kept the family together and on the right path. My dad worked to help others, while my mother worked to help my dad and their three children. You could say she was his sugar-mama, so to speak, and I say it with all the love and admiration that can be given to a woman who never complained and who has continued to work all her life in the interest of her family. She is a true hard-working woman who does it all. There are very few people who write as beautifully as my mother does, and I believe it is from her gift that my joy of writing flows.

I am and will be forever grateful to my mother for always being there for my sisters and me and showing her love unconditionally to this day.

To My Sisters

My sisters have shown me the love and understanding which can come only from family. They have encouraged me to be a better version of myself each day and accepted me for who I am in all my ways, which I have to say has not been normal by societal standards. My older sister, Marva, takes much from my father in being an extrovert and exceptional in her customer service expertise.

These days, customer service seems to have gone to the dogs in most businesses. However, one of Marva's callings is to help companies return to a level of service that can be admired and celebrated by all. She is certainly continuing that part of my father's legacy.

My younger sister, Nicole, speaks nine languages. With her modeling production company and agency for luxury and high net-worth clients, she brings her flare for extravagance to a new level. To many, it may appear quite a contradiction from my father's way of living, but I can say the focus for Nicole is to give people the luxury experience while ensuring she can share with everyone how best to live and be a better version of themselves each day. When she started her company, the slogan was "not just a pretty face," as she sought to look for models who also possessed inner beauty and purpose beyond their obvious external beauty. Nicole and I have begun to embark on a journey of self-discovery and one where we are a better version of ourselves each day; what better way to share with others? We do not preach; we show by being an example and a beacon of light, joy, confidence, and having a positive attitude in all we do. In a world of darkness, everyone should consider themselves as being the light. I am thankful to my sisters for the unique ways by which they share such joys with the world.

To My Daughter and Son

I am thankful to my children for being the most precious human beings. They show me great love and demonstrate values that make a father proud. My genius boy, who, being autistic and a cancer survivor (at 21 months old), has not withered away but has proven to be more thoughtful about life than many adults. He is now 15 years old and is one of the smartest people I know.

I look forward to him using his genius talents to help others. My daughter sings like an angel and melts my heart when she does, as well as all the other things she does, which makes a father proud. She and I took a road trip during the summer of 2022 from Montana to Nevada, and it was a week of getting to know the young lady she had become at 18 years old. It was one of the most rewarding trips I have ever taken.

I am thankful that both my children think of themselves as individuals first and always seek truth, love, peace, and understanding without being led astray by the limitations only they can put on themselves through acceptance of perceived societal norms. Like all of us, the power of God is within them, and I pray they choose to use that power for good, fulfilling their purpose, and living a meaningful life.

To My Wife

I thank my wife for recognizing that life is not fair and that we should always seek our path and purpose no matter how uncomfortable it may be. She has much to offer many. I know she has an inner spirit longing for truth. Our daughter's gift of singing comes from her mother and likely to a lesser extent from my father, as my wife sings even more beautifully. If she would only share this with the world, everyone would be mesmerized, enlightened, and inspired by her voice. The greatest gift she has given me is letting go, allowing me to be an inspiration to many and fulfill my purpose, and for that, I am and will always be forever grateful.

To Siedah Garrett

Before I met my wife, my first love was singer, songwriter, and record producer Deniece Williams, until I got to listen to Michael Jackson sing 'man in the mirror', a song co-written by Siedah Garrett. I soon after got to listen to Siedah sing the same song, and her words resonated with me since then. 34 years later, the song was the impetus for me to write this book. Excuses are an easy way for us to not look in the mirror and make the change that begins with us. Taking the first step to living a life of purpose with meaning, requires we all look in the mirror, take a look at ourselves and make the change. Essentially, change in the world begins with each one of us, and I am forever grateful to Siedah for being blessed to write such a beautiful song that has stood the test of time and has the same meaning today as it did when she wrote it.

Finally, To God

I thank God for mercy, grace, and the power of the mind and the spirit within me. Some call it the Holy Spirit; I call it "God within me." I denounce the purveyors of most organized religions for not holding to the fundamental underpinning of our existence: a purpose of service to others and knowing God intimately, not as a man, but as an energy force living within us all, in which we have the choice to select the path of service or the path of self-destruction. I choose the path of service, and it is all because my chosen belief in God has been strengthened through my knowledge and acceptance that we were born as the greatest masterpieces on earth; each person with individual gifts and talents, no matter what ailment or infirmity may befall us. The question is what we do with the hand we have been dealt: make lemonade out of lemons or let them stay and rot…such is our life, and it is the only one we have to live.

To All

My deepest thanks and love to all. May this book be a blessing of encouragement and inspiration to all who seek to live a better life: a life of purpose with meaning.

I'm too old!
I'm waiting for the right opportunity
I'm not educated enough
Life is not fair
I'm not ready
NME
NO MORE EXCUSE

INTRODUCTION

The title "No More Excuses" lays the foundation of the entire book, as each chapter includes examples of the excuses many give daily without realizing. Doing so is just a way of avoiding taking the next step to fulfilling a life of purpose with meaning. It begins with believing in yourself, and knowing your purpose, followed by setting a goal to walk fervently in the light of possibilities, acknowledging that the greatest power in the universe is your mind which you've been given freely from birth. You have infinite reasons for not doing what needs to be done. You can give a myriad of excuses for any failure. Any time you give up and put something off for tomorrow, there is always an excuse ready to abdicate yourself of all and any responsibility. It is easy. It is lethal. It is fatal to your purpose and deadly to all meaning in your life.

The purpose of this book is not to attempt to force a specific philosophy or thought down your throat. There is no pulpit or cult or desire to gather followers. Instead, I seek to live a life of purpose by not making excuses, highlighting why excuses are poison to the soul and hopefully, this will resonate with many and encourage you to take the first step to living a life of purpose with meaning, as your journey is an individual one, void of group identity and conformity. This book's purpose is simple - to help you work towards a meaningful and purposeful life.

Now, the natural thing is to ask the simple question-what is your purpose, anyway? Well, the answer is also quite simple. Everyone, quite literally everyone, has only one purpose: to serve others.

Most of what we do, as human beings, has to do with other people. In an office, retail, or in a manufacturing plant, we work towards creating and transporting goods to people—serving them in that way. We may also create value by working in the service industry - an industry built quite literally on providing service to others, whether directly or indirectly.

It might be difficult for many to accept the fact that their sole purpose in life is to serve others. However, the reality is that many people do not actually understand what "purpose" means or what "meaning" is. Many people think the two are one and the same - which is not the case. Meaning is the contentment that enters your life when you are working honestly towards fulfilling your purpose—that is all.

Since your purpose is to serve others, you must find meaning by fulfilling your purpose in the way you were meant to do. While everyone's primary purpose is to serve others, each is destined to do so in different ways. These different ways are through the skills, talents, gifts, and affinities everyone has towards different kinds of work. Some find cooking meaningful; for others, it is improving a business or starting something new. Some are content with doing the same task repeatedly, and others can only find happiness whilst learning new things and attaining new skills.

In any case, your purpose is to serve others in some way, shape, or form. If everyone recognized their purpose and worked towards achieving such with meaning, the world would be a far more harmonious place.

Unfortunately, the grim reality of the world is that many people seldom, if ever, uncover their talents or skills throughout their lives. I should mention that, for simplicity, I will use the words talents and gifts together or by themselves, so forgive me for not acknowledging the difference each time. We were all born with certain talents which some call gifts. Skills, on the other hand, are often taught. However, whether I use the words talents, gifts, or skills, all of them require that we nurture and harness them, or else they will never be used effectively in the pursuit of living a life of purpose with meaning.

People are often stuck trying to fit a square peg in a round hole and trying to find meaning without being able to do so. Many are pushed towards some things while being pushed away from others due to the forces of the market, family pressures, and the considerations of society itself. A talented gardener with a green thumb may be stuck working in a factory, and a talented linguist might use his/her skills to scam others rather than be motivated to do something good and worthwhile.

It is thus not a surprise that most people dislike their jobs, and there are high rates of depression and anxiety across the globe. These individuals are stuck living unfulfilling lives and depart from this world without being able to pursue their true purpose in the way they were meant to.

Consider this book the kick you need to get going on the journey of walking into the light to live a life of purpose with meaning. I mentioned some of the many excuses you might have to stop you from pursuing your true purpose, and in this book, you will find rebuttals to every single one.

So, let's begin!

1

"I'M WAITING ON GOD FOR A SIGN"

"Many stay inactive waiting on God, when it is God who is waiting on them to listen, then act accordingly, as faith without works is dead."

One of the most debilitating excuses you have is to "wait for a sign," or "hang on for the right time," or something equally superstitious. It is one of the unfortunate by-products of the indoctrination espoused by the purveyors of most organized religions.

Now, I believe that waiting on God for a sign is not religious, but it is definitely based on superstition disguised as religion. Think of it this way: many will say to you that you should keep praying, and God will show you the way. However, many never tell you that prayer requires faith, and faith without works is dead. Why is that? Well, most base their thoughts on superstition, which has little to no validity, but given that they are controlled by such things, they never open their minds to the possibility of the power from within themselves and that the God whom they serve has made them special in many ways with gifts and talents to do extraordinary things, if they only truly believed in themselves. For example, many Christians quote a passage of the Bible from Philippians 4:13, which says, "I can do all things through Christ who strengthens me". Now, if they truly believed in what they were saying, every action would be without fear, without doubt, and a manifestation of their faith in the masterpiece which they were created to be.

Unfortunately, the lack of self-belief, surrounded by fear, doubt, and overall superstition, will hold you back from striving toward your true purpose and achieving any kind of meaning in life.

This is not intended as a statement against religion; but as more of a warning against buying into the indoctrination of the purveyors of religion themselves; the people who stand on pulpits promising you the world and giving you false hope while filling their coffers in return. The truth is, life is not fair and none of them know exactly what will happen to you if you pray or not pray, if you believe in what they are saying or do not, if you do exactly what they tell you to do over and over again. If they knew, they would be God, and you and I know they are not. Therefore, why do they seem to have all the answers to life's mysteries or just throw their hands in the air and say "trust God" and apologize for the fact that your prayers are not answered in the way that you want? You waste your time, resources, and effort helping them rather than finding your own purpose and working towards finding true meaning in your life. That is what God wants from each of us, which is to live a life of purpose. At the pearly gates, if you believe in such a thing, I firmly believe you will not be asked about how many times you went to church or prayed, but what you DID with your life in fulfillment of your purpose of serving others. Again, I believe prayer is essential in demonstrating your belief in God and the Power from within, but nothing is as important as having faith in the fact that you were born with gifts and talents to be used to do extraordinary things in pursuit of living a life of purpose with meaning. Many pray, but do they have faith to actually go out and fulfill a life of purpose, or do they remain waiting on God for a sign?

God does not provide conditional help, nor does He wish to work miracles to help those who simply go to church or pray in general. There is a saying that God helps those who help themselves. While this saying can be argued, it is rarely argued that only by actively demonstrating one's faith, that those who recognize real-life opportunities and use their God-given gifts and talents toward fulfilling their true purpose in their own ways can succeed. Many people find purpose from God and are helped through their closeness to religious beliefs, but many tend to forget, or do not know, the concept of using their talents and working hard and smart to achieve something of value. They keep waiting for a "sign from God" to help guide them towards success, even though the sign has been within them all along.

The talents and skills we have, in themselves, are gifts from God, or just gifts if you do not believe in God, as irrespective of your beliefs, one thing is certain, we were all born with certain gifts, talents, and skills, and our life's journey is meant to uncover, embrace, harness, and nurture such gifts to fulfill our purpose. The time we have and the energy we have are blessings which allow us to practice and nurture those talents. One thing is for sure, and that is, our talents are given to us free at birth, while skills must be taught. However, it is extremely important to note that both talents and skills require nurturing and harnessing to have any chance of being used to live a life of purpose with meaning.

Instead of waiting for God to show us our purpose, we must improve ourselves so we are prepared when opportunities come and are able to fulfill our purpose in life. Some call it "in God's time," but the most important truth to note is that no one gets to the point of success by making excuses. Nor can anyone achieve their goals without visualizing those goals and making every effort to achieve them. It is a fallacy to think that praying alone will work towards achieving anything in life, as prayer requires faith, and faith without works is dead. Ultimately, you need to understand that the next step after faith is to go out and do what is needed to achieve anything you want in life and to use the skills that you have in the service of others, thus fulfilling your purpose and doing so with meaning.

When you serve others by providing a service, manufacturing a product, helping someone in need, or listening to someone who wants to be heard, how can life not be meaningful? In my experience, I have found it extremely rewarding to go above and beyond in my job responsibilities or in meeting customer needs than to just do the bare minimum. In recent times, I have seen a deterioration in the quality of service in almost every service industry. Why is that? Well, it appears that many are just filling a position and working to earn a dollar, to make ends meet, to feed themselves and, in some cases, their families, and nothing more. No one with such an attitude should have an expectation of being promoted or moving up the ladder, or going out on their own with a business venture. Not with such laissez-faire attitudes. Surprisingly, these are usually the ones who complain about their jobs the most, despite doing very little to showcase their talents, if they even know or believe they have such talents in the first place. They expect the money to come first, and their efforts at work will follow. During that time, many are just waiting on God for a sign to leave the job or do something else. This seems like a failing attitude to me, as how can they ever expect to achieve anything great when the little things, such as doing the best they can with the current job they have as they work out a plan to achieve their goals, are not given priority? Some may ask, what if they do not want to do anything great? My response is, why not? You will find the reason why many do not even consider doing anything great is because they do not recognize the power that lies within them, and many are still waiting on God for a sign.

My father was the funniest man I have ever known and a great storyteller. When I was a young boy, he told me the following story of a man on a rooftop.

There was a man who lived alone in a small town. One day, the rains came, and the entire town was in danger of flooding. Most people began to evacuate, but the man remained. He was asked by the authorities to vacate his premises, as the flood was likely to be fatal.

His reply was, "God will help me."

The authorities asked that he leave and get to higher ground, but he insisted there was no reason for him to leave, as God would never let him die.

Even his friends passed by his house on their way to the safety of the higher ground and begged him to leave, yet he did not leave. The water began to rise and soon reached the top floor. The man still insisted God would save him, and he managed to climb onto the roof. What happened next was nothing short of a miracle, since everyone in the town had left their homes to get to safety. Some men in a boat passed by and offered to take him to safety, yet the man declined their offer.

Next, a large branch from a fallen tree floated by the man, yet the man pushed it away, saying, "God will save me." Finally, a helicopter passed by; seeing the man on the roof, they threw down a rope for him to climb on so they could take him to safety, yet the man declined, saying, "God will save me." Well, the man drowned, and at the gates of heaven, the man asked, "God, I have been faithful for many years, I have given to the poor, I have been loving to my family, I have tried to live a good life, and I have always attended to those in need; why did you not help me when I needed you most?"

- God looked at the man and said…. "You fool,
- I told the town folk to tell you to leave,
- I sent men on a boat to help you,
- I sent a log from a tree to help you.
- I also sent a helicopter to help you, yet you denied my help you FOOL."

The same is true for us when we do not realize what is in front of us or fail to listen to the voice we hear in the stillness of the night, during our daily lives, or in our times of need. Some may ask, "What does this story have to do with everyday life?" My only response is that I see it every day, and so do you. Let me share with you just one of my many observations in my life that demonstrate how such excuses can be debilitating.

John is one of my acquaintances who has lost quite a lot throughout the years, as he constantly gets into debt due to his gambling problem. However, over more than 40 years, many of his close friends and family have continued to pray for him. He also prays for God to heal him and stop what he calls an uncontrollable urge to gamble. However, over the years, many people, including myself, have offered to take him to special meetings for gamblers so that he can get the help he needs. We have often offered to cut all of his credit cards and put him on a strict budget. We have also left pamphlets and sent strangers who are ex-gamblers, to help him, yet he found a reason to depend on God to save him from himself. He still has not changed. He continues to make excuses for falling into the trap that he puts himself, gambling all his earned money and racking up debt, only to do it all over again and again once he has earned more money or has eased himself from the stress of debt. The point here is that John continues to wait on God when the signs have been there in many ways, but he refuses to heed the call to action.

This is the reason why as you read this book, to succeed in life in immeasurable ways, you must be willing to open your eyes, look in the mirror and be prepared to make the necessary changes, recognizing that the signs and answers to save yourself from the chains of fear and doubt are and have always been around you, but such chains are yours to unlock and be free. It is not the absence of fear and doubt, but your ability to choose to step in faith in spite of fear and doubt. In short, we must have the courage to persevere. If you do not face such fears, there will be no hope for your transformation of leaving the past behind you, embracing the magnificent you, and allowing that wonderful individual to step into the light of success and freedom from all such bad habits. I know this is not easy to do, but nothing worthwhile is ever easy, so please do not make another excuse saying to me, "you don't understand. It is not easy to get rid of this habit." The more you say that it is not easy to do something, the more difficult it is, as it becomes a self-fulfilling prophecy perpetuated by your mind to keep you from your own joy. No one will save you from these ailments; it is all within you to make the necessary changes in your life, to not hold on to the warm embrace of excuses which eventually burn into your flesh and cause you to live an unfulfilled life.

Opportunity and assistance are presented daily in our lives, but we are blinded by false doctrines and superstitions instead of freeing our minds to use common sense and our intellect above all, as God expects us to do. We overlook opportunities which seem "ordinary," believing we should wait on God for the "extraordinary." In doing so, we miss the stepping stones of assistance laid down in our path daily and leave God waiting on us to choose a path and act accordingly. My friend and mentor, Madelyn, once told me that people often confuse waiting on God with working with God, and that is the lazy person's way of pretending to be faithful. Don't let that be you, as you were not born to be lazy, but to show your faith by doing what you know should, and can, be done to live a life of purpose with meaning.

My wish is for us to live a life of purpose, using our talents and gifts to serve others while acknowledging that we were born not to wait on God, as God is the one who is waiting on us to live a fulfilled and meaningful life. When our time comes, let us hope we are not called FOOLS.

If you wish for the same, then learn to recognize what you have as blessings from God and use those blessings to pursue your purpose and find meaning in your life. Divine intervention is not something you should wait for; rather, it is something you should seize when it is God's time, which is almost always now. You should work and stay true to yourself the way God intended rather than seeking "signs" or something equally superstitious to guide you.

Remember, it is an insult to wait on God when God has created such a masterpiece in you and is waiting on YOU to choose to live a life of purpose with meaning.

The choice is yours!

I wish I could run the Marathon, but I'm too old!
FINISH

2

"I'M TOO OLD"

"You are never too old to set another goal or dream a new dream, and act on it."
C.S. Lewis

Writer Harry Bernstein authored countless books, all rejected, before getting his first bestseller, The Invisible Wall: A Love Story That Broke Barriers, at age ninety-six. Henry Ford found success with the Model T at forty-six. Stan Lee, the father of the most iconic and successful comic and movie empire of the Marvel franchise, created the Fantastic Four at thirty-eight and worked into his nineties. They did not sit down and complain that they were too old to change or believe they could not achieve success past a certain age. They got up each morning and worked to pursue their passions and achieve their purpose.

The average man simply does not do so. Why? Lack of momentum is the reason.

Momentum is a concept in physics where an object tends to remain in its state of movement, so momentum is the quantity of motion. Momentum is often defined as mass in motion—each of us has mass, and if we are moving, we have momentum, thus mass in motion. The term momentum is often used regarding sports teams on winning streaks, an army that seems unstoppable, or an executive successfully climbing the corporate ladder.

In overcoming a lack of momentum, I do not want to diminish the importance that having a positive attitude plays in taking your first step towards a life of meaning. Such an attitude can only come from realizing your purpose and using your talents and gifts to pursue a meaningful life.

However, the key to understanding and achieving momentum is that people often take a first step and a second and then stop at the third, or somewhere along the way, once they are faced with obstacles or challenges. Essentially, they give up, get older, and then use their age as an excuse for not living a fulfilled life. Momentum is necessary to pursue the actions required to achieve life's goals and continue striving toward a meaningful, fulfilling life.

Another phenomenon which might make the idea of momentum more relatable (though for the wrong reasons) is known as the "sunk cost fallacy." Sunk cost fallacy is when a person keeps going with the same losing strategy in life because they do not want to admit that the money, time, and work they've put into it were a waste. They will not change their behavior for fear of looking dumb or stupid to others. They do not want to say they put in all that effort for nothing.

The two concepts are completely different, but often confused. When used to pursue one's goals, momentum is extremely important to achieving them, whereas the sunk cost fallacy, even with momentum, leads to nowhere.

Both momentum and the sunk cost fallacy come into play whenever you hear the excuse "I am too old" in relation to choosing to do what brings you great joy without fear and doubt and taking the steps needed to live a life of purpose with meaning. Momentum is required to not give up. Sunk cost fallacy is not allowing momentum to get in the way of stopping those things which aren't working and taking the risks required to do the things you've always wanted to do but are too afraid to admit you should have done so many years ago.

If we have learned anything, it is that you are never too old to start. There is a famous saying, "an old dog cannot learn new tricks," but thankfully, people are not dogs and are bestowed with amazing minds, more creative and powerful than a dog can ever be. The truth is, old dogs can learn new tricks, so how much more can intelligent and creative humans like us learn? As many new tricks as we want. All that is required is the ability to believe in ourselves and the desire to put in the work! We find no success in achieving our goals without putting in the effort and knowing that the effort without momentum is futile.

Now, back to physics and the concept of momentum—the more time we spend doing something, the easier it gets. More importantly, with momentum, we will face greater difficulty in changing such an action as it becomes a positive habit. If we get used to spending most of our life being a certain way, it will take energy to change it. We need to remember here that it can be changed. The power is in us to change, but only if we believe we can!

The biggest meteors hurtling through space, backed by incredible amounts of momentum, can be redirected with a smaller application of force. The proper angle, the correct force, and a change with redirection can happen.

The same applies to your life; if you are older and have been hurtling along at the same rate for a long time, you do not have to continue hurtling aimlessly. It is never too late to turn your life around or move in a different direction.

Yes, there will come a time when it will be too late - when you are dead. There will be plenty of time to rest when you are six feet under, plenty of time. The point is, as long as you breathe and have the use of your mind, you can change.

Our capacity to change is one of our greatest blessings in this life. You can use it as an opportunity to work toward becoming a better version of yourself each day. As long as you are alive, you owe it to yourself not to die with regrets of never having pursued your dreams and used your talents and skills with meaning and passion in the service of others.

Comfort is the enemy of change. People get used to the routine a job, a hobby, a habit, or a certain way of living provides them. Some may say that they cannot be blamed, as familiarity, comfort, and the relative safety which comes with routine feel good. Putting a safe, secure way of life at risk and taking a leap of faith can be a huge challenge that is very difficult for many people to imagine. However, when you consider the alternative of not pursuing your dreams, what are you left with?

Then again, there is the question of why.

You might find yourself asking, "Why would I want things to change?"

The answer is quite simple. If you are living a life of purpose and are fulfilled and joyful, then you need not change at all. But therein is where the rubber hits the road, does it not?

Do you have zero regrets because you are doing what you are most passionate about? Would you continue to do what you are currently doing if you won the lottery or if money were not a concern? If your answer is 'yes' to both these questions, I'd say we have found in you an individual who is one in a billion. In most cases, many people have a hobby, a business idea, or an endeavor they want to pursue, which gives them a greater purpose. In many instances, it is a dream they have held for years, but one from which they have shut themselves off as they aged. It is an unfortunate position, and it should not be the case.

It is true that certain restraints come with age and are very real. For example, you cannot play effectively or even be accepted in the NBA at the age of sixty—that is certain. The reality of the situation is way too common for many people. As people get older, they age more in their minds because they tell themselves they are simply too old to pursue their passions or fulfill their dreams. They capture and imprison themselves, continually telling their minds that they cannot step out of their self-imposed prison to find their purpose.

However, one of the great aspects of being human is that once we have been shown something, however improbable, is possible, we can start working toward that goal or purpose. It took a long time for the first man to break the four-minute mile, and now people do it routinely. The first person who achieved a winter ascent of K-2 was told it was impossible, and now there are multiple individuals who have accomplished what was once deemed "impossible."

To hammer home the point that it is indeed never too late to find your purpose, let's look at Liang Huguo. Liang hails from Yunnan, China, and he has one of the most inspiring stories of finding his passion at a later age. Most people in their fifties, and some in their forties, think their final score is on the board. They believe they have entered the last leg of their lives, and all they could do has been done. They begin to consider retirement, wondering if it is even possible. They think of comfort. Not so for Liang, who, at the ripe old age of seventy, decided to try something new. He took up running in the golden years of his life, and immediately found he liked it. He was passionate. Liang focused on what he loved, eating simple, running smart, and caring for his body overall. In 2018, within two years of pursuing his new passion, he had run seventy-two marathons.

Most people might just want to complete a marathon, but he completed seventy-two and was even able to achieve a sub four-hour marathon—a difficult feat for athletes who have not specialized in endurance. Liang's example is extreme, but it serves as a solid, straightforward purpose and example: when people say they are too old to do something, it is very likely because they believe they are too old.

The belief is not founded in fact, because you are seldom ever too old to fulfill your dreams and live a meaningful and joyful life. It is important to note that Liang's story is one of not giving up. It is a story of a man who found his passion for running by believing in himself. He is doing what he is passionate about, but this does not necessarily mean he has found his purpose. A full, contented life is more than fulfilling childhood dreams or checking off items on a bucket list. Mr. Huguo's life story is a tale of inspiration and an example of not giving up and not using an excuse to avoid taking charge of your life to the detriment of living your purpose.

For the most part, experience comes with age and should be celebrated, yet doing so requires the older person to use life's experiences to fulfill their purpose. It all comes down to having the right mindset. Age becomes just a number for those who have the proper mindset and pursue their dreams with passion at any age. Many people throughout history have demonstrated their resolve to achieve what others much younger than them could only hope to accomplish.

It really is all about having the right mindset, as the familiar adage reminds us, "you are only as old as you feel." It is not far from the truth. As we get older, our agility declines, but even then, it should not be acceptable to speed up our decline with a negative, defeatist mindset.

The word 'feel' in the adage comes from our thoughts and mindset. The more we convince ourselves we are old, the more we use it as an excuse, and the more it becomes a reality in everything we do. Not a single person in history who accomplished their goals when they were older had a mindset that they could not achieve the goal they set out to reach. A famous proverb declares, "For as a man thinketh in his heart, so is he." A truer and more powerful statement I could not make.

I often tell my daughter, "If you say you can't do something, then you can't. If you say you can do something, you can and you will, as the mind allows the body to do what is necessary to achieve what it believes."

I acknowledge that there are times when you fail to achieve, even when you say you can. This is when the courage, commitment, and perseverance to never give up comes into play. Too often, people give up at the first sign of failure. It is the reason there are more failures than successes in life—it is far easier to give up than to press on and keep doing what you believe is possible.

It is simpler to say you are too old than to take steps to achieve what you want. In taking the needed steps, you must go at your own pace, not at the pace of others, as life's journey is just as sweet and often even sweeter than life's destinations. In history, there are great examples of people who accomplished great things as they got older. Colonel Sanders was sixty-five years old when he started KFC. Teiichi Igarashi climbed Japan's tallest mountain at the age of one hundred. John Glenn, the first American to orbit the Earth, went into space again at age seventy-seven. In doing so, they joined a very long list of individuals who achieved extraordinary accomplishments in their golden years rather than making excuses.

The principle of momentum dictates that an object stays in its existing state until a force is applied to change its state. Consider this the force you need to start your life rolling in a different and more positive direction.

Having read about those who had successes later in life, I ask you, "What is your excuse?"

If you think you are too old, you might want to think again. Better years are only steps away if you accept that the time is now to make the moves toward living a life of purpose with meaning. After all, your experiences have brought you thus far in life for a reason, so grab hold of all that is possible and live a better life going forward. You deserve it!

The choice is yours!

MA
MBBS
BED
MTECH
CBSC
CAT
MSC
UPSC
IBPS
LLB
MBA
BA
BARCH
NIT

3

"I'M NOT EDUCATED ENOUGH"

"Education is the passport to the future, for tomorrow belongs to those who prepare for it today."
~ Malcolm X

Having an education is among the most crucial and significant deciding factors when it comes to a successful future.

However, we need to temper the desire for what is deemed "education" with reality, as using this excuse can be extremely dangerous, because it is a lie wrapped in logic. We've been taught our entire lives that more education is better than less, and this may be a lie, as education is usually considered in the form of formal schooling.

In general, many people think that more is always better. Consider the following lies:

More security is always better for us.

More money is always better for us.

More education is always better for us.

These are all lies. What people don't realize is that more than a mouthful can be a waste, and what matters is not having more, but what you do with the "little" of the "more" that you have—and education is no exception. More education is NOT always better for us, depending on our skills and where our passion lies.

There was a study done and published in the Journal of Applied Psychology (1 March 2017), on the relationship between IQ and leadership. The researchers wanted to find out if smarter people made better leaders, and what they discovered shocked everyone. To their surprise, the researchers discovered that people's leadership ability actually decreased when they scored an IQ above 120.

Let that sink in for a moment.

The report noted that an IQ above 126 actually reduced a person's leadership ability. And what does that mean? Well, if it means anything, it means that more education, in the traditional sense, is NOT always better for us. What we've failed to realize is that education is subject to the law of diminishing returns. The law of diminishing returns states that more is not always better. There comes a point where education actually gets in the way of your ability to lead and be creative. However, the point here is not whether intelligent people make good leaders or are the most successful, but that there is a point where more education in a formal setting never equates to more success. Hopefully, I will be successful in explaining further through actual accounts of success and the reasons why you should stop thinking that your one degree, multiple degrees, or no degree is not enough and a detriment to your success.

After age, not having a degree or a certain level of education is one of the most prevalent excuses individuals use for not setting goals or following their dreams. Doing so shifts the blame from them and instead makes it all about their circumstances. Sadly, a lack of education then becomes an acceptable excuse for both society and individuals.

We need to stop and ask ourselves what it truly means to be educated. Does education mean having a piece of paper declaring we are educated, or does education mean having acquired a certain level of knowledge?

You see, there is an immensely important factor which needs to be considered whenever education is being discussed, nay, whenever it is even thought about. Education is often conflated with having earned a degree or certification. However, this is a false narrative and a negative worldview which needs to be changed so more people can truly pursue their dreams.

In many circles, you are considered educated if you have attended college or an institute of higher learning. Having a certificate or degree is one sign you did indeed attend college and/or university and you are educated at a certain level. A higher level of education is often held in high regard by potential employers, but in truth, school is not the be-all and end-all of education.

There is a myriad of avenues for acquiring knowledge which can bring success and allow you to pursue your dreams. Mark Twain offered similar advice: "Do not let school get in the way of your education." He was right.

Many people do not need a degree to become successful and achieve their dreams. I am not saying you should ditch school, but rather, you should seek to use your gifts in pursuit of your passion. Your passion is only known by you when you embrace the power within and take the leap of faith, like many successful people before you have done.

When someone tells you they are not educated enough to accomplish their goals, you should ask, "How much more education do you need to succeed?" Often, they have not considered the level of education they already possess, or the level they believe is required to achieve their goals. Do they really understand what they want, or is it expressed simply as an excuse for not putting in the work needed to succeed?

I am not saying you should not seek to be educated, but often, people mistake schooling for education. Education, though not necessarily through schooling, is the path many successful entrepreneurs took - a path by which they did not use their lack of multiple degrees as the reason why they could not succeed or even as an excuse for simply not trying to succeed.

The point is this—you should seek to be educated, but not necessarily schooled. Schooling is the formal acquisition of knowledge. Education is life's acquisition of knowledge. More than half of the most successful people did not finish formal schooling but had a vision and determination to learn, thus educating themselves and ultimately achieving greater success in the process.

The lesson for us all is to not use the lack of a degree (schooling) as the reason or excuse for not succeeding; instead, take the steps needed for the genuine education needed to achieve your goals and dreams. Formal schooling provides you with the basic requirements to take your education to the next level. One should never assume that education ends once one has graduated, as that would be false and lead to mediocrity and seldom to succeeding at anything worthwhile.

Entrepreneurial success is more prevalent in the modern age, where access to all manner of knowledge is cheaply and often freely available to everyone. Formal institutes of learning do not hold a monopoly over the definition of what can be considered an education. In fact, more and more data are available which show that certain types of schooling are restrictive to a person's imaginative, innovative, and creative capabilities.

Think about those who attended high school and college and went on to regular jobs. What traits did they develop during their formal schooling that had the most impact on their success within those rigid structures? Was it their creativity? Was it their innovation? Was it their IQ?

No. Rather, it was simply how good they were at following orders. It is in line with older generations when children were trained to follow orders and do as they were told. The truth is, formal education is meant only for a select few whose dreams align with what they learn; the rest simply follow along, hoping for the best, without any set goal or dream in mind.

In light of this fact, it is no wonder so many highly educated people abandon their dreams, fearful of what they may risk to achieve what they want. They end up being intellectually imprisoned all their lives.

Furthermore, many of our modern school systems have become out of touch regarding technology and have become more about keeping students entertained and/or trapped in the mission to keep everyone at the level of the least of these students in aptitude to not offend anyone.

This skewed structure creates students who do not know how to think critically. In addition, it limits the creativity, ingenuity, and freedom of those who have demonstrated a higher aptitude and results in the perpetuation of students who believe they need more schooling. In truth, students need more education and the freedom to unleash the power within; none of which is found in most institutions of higher learning.

I hope this provides you with one crucial lesson: whether you are highly educated or not, you can still follow your dreams and aspirations and lead a successful and fulfilling life.

Every time you hear yourself or someone else say, "I am not educated enough," in relation to trying something different or pursuing a dream, think about what is really meant by making such a statement.

Do they mean they do not know enough about a particular topic? Do they mean they do not have a degree or certification? If it is either, the easy rebuttal is as we already stated—you can educate yourself in anything as long as you have access to the internet to research what experts have written. You can also speak to those who are experts in the area in which you feel you lack knowledge, or you can pursue working in the field/industry to get a better understanding of the area that most interests you. It is as simple as that, but often, it requires sacrifice which many people seldom wish to make.

There are so many free resources online that contain so many different topics that you can learn what you need to know to begin pursuing your dreams. As long as you can read, breathe, and have use of your mind, you can learn any skill you want and start pursuing the dream you want to achieve. Imagine if Bill Gates, Mark Zuckerberg, Steve Jobs, Richard Branson, and many others used such an excuse and did not follow their dreams and passion. Imagine if they all used the excuse that they could not start a business because they did not have a university degree.

There are paths set in stone for people to follow, and then there are paths that need to be made by those who want to achieve their dreams by any means necessary. Some are given the path to follow by way of inheritance, others by having supportive parents or the right mentor. On the other hand, there are those who must look deep within and create their own path. The point we must all understand is that nothing should keep us from finding our path, even if we were not born with the proverbial silver spoon.

When you have the passion and determination to take the first step and assume the risks, to use the skills you have to step out in faith, great things can happen, even if you do not succeed the first time. You only need to keep working on getting the knowledge required to get where you need and want to be. If your dream is to own a business, you can learn the required skills online or as an apprentice. If your dream is to get a better job, you can determine the skills needed and work on improving those skills for yourself. It is simply a question of determination. As the proverb states, "where there is a will, there is indeed a way."

The determination and commitment to never give up and not make excuses for one's circumstances is what separates true success from constant failure and ongoing regret.

So, should the "I am not educated enough" excuse ever be used? The answer is a resounding NO.

Maybe you cannot learn everything online, but there is much to be said about the importance of on-the-job experience in the way of education. Bill Gates began Microsoft, and through his learning experiences and practical knowledge, he built the world's largest personal computer software company.

The lesson here is to not think of education as only going to school, but as seeking your passion through the skills and talents you have. It is doing everything in your power to continue improving your craft and your skill, as no formal education will ever prepare you to fully be your very best.

Benjamin Franklin left school at ten years old. He went on to work around that fact, using books and his own curiosity to become one of the most famous inventors and innovators of all time. His lack of education never held him back.

I am not saying you should not go to school, but you should not feel you need multiple degrees and designations to do what you are passionate about and to live your life with purpose. The only person who will stand in your way is you.

The choice is yours!

4

"I'M WAITING FOR THE RIGHT OPPORTUNITY"

"Opportunity is missed by most people because it is dressed in overalls and looks like work."
~ Thomas A. Edison

It sounds like something a smart person would say, doesn't it? After all, being selective with our time and energy is intelligent, wouldn't you say? When we say that we are waiting for the right opportunity, what we are really doing is weaponizing our own language against ourselves. As Wittgenstein said, "language disguises thoughts". It's not that we are waiting for the right opportunity, it is that we are afraid of being embarrassed. We live in a world where videos of people failing are more popular than videos of people succeeding. It turns out, most people are just waiting to laugh at others and gossip to their friends for a glimpse of attention. Don't lie to yourself. You can lie to your mom, your dad, your sister, your brother, and even your husband or wife, but you cannot lie to yourself. You can ignore yourself, but you cannot lie to yourself. You are not waiting for the right opportunity; you are waiting for life to get easier.

Today, this ends. You are not going to wait for life to get easier any longer. You are not going to wait for the right opportunity any longer. Why? Because opportunity is cultivated. Opportunity is harvested. It is extremely important to understand this critical point.

When a baseball player hits a home run, what makes the home run possible? Is it the pitcher's mistake or the batter's prowess, skill, and attention? The truth is, it is both. A prepared batter in baseball is one who is ready for a pitcher to make a mistake, essentially being prepared to take advantage of an opportunity. So, it is where preparation meets opportunity, and that is why waiting for the right opportunity is so damaging to your success.

When you are presented with an opportunity, the opportunity is successfully embraced by your preparedness. If luck is when opportunity meets preparedness, you cannot get lucky if you are not prepared. Therefore, opportunity presents itself to those who have prepared themselves for such an opportunity. Unprepared people seem to never catch a break...just the way the universe intended.

I also often think about the story in the bible where David kills Goliath. The reference to David and Goliath has been used worldwide to highlight small versus big. However, when I think of David, I think of him as being prepared to meet Goliath in battle, since he would not have been successful if he had not had the experience of using a sling before. This is best described in the following passages from the bible:

David said to Saul, "Let no one lose heart on account of this Philistine; your servant will go and fight him."

Saul replied, "You are not able to go out against this Philistine and fight him; you are only a young man, and he has been a warrior from his youth."

But David said to Saul, "Your servant has been keeping his father's sheep. When a lion or a bear came and carried off a sheep from the flock, I went after it, struck it and rescued the sheep from its mouth. When it turned on me, I seized it by its hair, struck it and killed it. Your servant has killed both the lion and the bear; this uncircumcised Philistine will be like one of them, because he has defied the armies of the living God. The Lord who rescued me from the paw of the lion and the paw of the bear will rescue me from the hand of this Philistine." (1 Samuel 17: 32-37)

Most of all, David had faith that he could slay Goliath and that he was prepared to do so. Do you have faith in your ability to achieve your goals and be prepared to do so when opportunities come your way? That is the question and what I hope to clear in your mind by the time you finish this chapter.

In the preceding chapters, we discussed the idea of people being risk-averse in their own unique ways. Sometimes people are risk-averse even when they have nothing really going on in their lives.

The reality is that many opportunities do come knocking throughout our lives, but they seldom bust the door open and wake us up. They come, they knock, but they do not wait for long.

You need to be able to seize the opportunity when it presents itself in your life, but you also need to be ready to work hard and work smart to get where you want and need to go.

Often, people do not even recognize an opportunity for what it is; they are simply not in the state of readiness needed to look for and see opportunities in the first place. Many times, the problem tends to be that people say they are looking for the "right opportunity," but they often wait so long the years pass them by, and they find it is too late.

The truth is, there is often no such thing as a "right opportunity" as many people picture it, so they find themselves waiting for a unique set of circumstances which never actually come.

You need to understand that opportunities must be seized when they come and created when they don't. Too many people live believing that if they jump, the risk might be too great and they might lose what they already have, so they stand still, preferring to play it safe. This kind of thinking, while understandable, often leads to a life full of regret. Most people who live life this way spend the rest of their lives wondering if things would have been better had they taken the risk.

You need to think about the sheer number of people who, when asked about their biggest regrets in their old age, say they wished they could have known what would have happened had they taken the road less traveled. They wonder what would have happened had they decided to risk it all in pursuit of their dreams—quitting their job to start their own business, asking their crush on a date, or pursuing the passion closest to their hearts.

There is often safety and stability in a cookie-cutter job and life, but it can simply not provide you with the sort of happiness and contentment which comes from following your dreams. Whether it be a new business, a better relationship, a once-in-a-lifetime trip, or a successful career, if the idea of failure or rejection is holding you back or if the risk seems to be overwhelming, then you need to start working on removing these self-imposed restraints from your mindset.

The truth is, people often exaggerate the possible risks in their own minds, not understanding that, quite often, they stand to gain a lot more than they stand to lose. Often, the kind of failure they are so afraid of is easy to recover from, and they end up discounting the immense learning opportunities that failures bring. They often end up being in a losing battle in a war they could have won had they dared enough to keep fighting.

To sum it up, perfectionism, at least in most areas, can cause you to become stagnant. If you stand still, waiting for the right opportunity to make the jump, hedging all possible bets, you might end up never jumping at all.

Everyone who has ever achieved success has had at least one or more instances in their lives where they had to take a jump, not knowing if they were going to land on their feet or fall flat on their backs but believing that taking the jump would be worth it. It made no sense taking the leap of faith by jumping with fear and doubt in their heart and not believing in the possible. These people had to believe that they could in order to succeed.

In fact, fear and doubt are the direct opposite of faith. You cannot say you have faith yet possess fear and doubt to act. Even if you have fear and doubt, one has to have the courage to proceed anyway, kicking fear and doubt aside with the right mindset. You either have faith that you can do the possible, or you think you can't do the possible and therefore call it impossible.

All who say they can't never believe it is possible. To have such a belief, one must have faith in the power from within, whether you believe it to be God or not, as, irrespective of your belief, such power lies in all of us.

"In a world that's changing really quickly, the only strategy that is guaranteed to fail is not taking risks," says Mark Zuckerberg, co-founder of Facebook and Meta Platforms. Taking chances and facing uncertainties are essential steps to following your dreams—otherwise, you would not dream.

We can look at the field of finance and find solid examples of the truth about taking risks and facing uncertainties. For example, investing in a government bond or T-Bills is low risk. It is certain to give you the return you have been promised, and there is stability in it as an investment. However, the return will generally be lower when compared with other investments. This is what is known as low-risk and low-reward. The two go hand in hand. Since most people are risk-averse, T-Bills are popular options for people to invest in safely.

Then, there are single-company stocks, cryptocurrencies, or other riskier assets. These can go up or down, and the return is not set in stone. You might make a lot or lose it all. This is, as expected, known as high-risk and high reward. You are often rewarded for taking a higher risk than most people. At the same time, the likelihood of a loss is also high.

Similarly, there is a level of uncertainty with which you will have to contend and extra work you will have to do in order to pursue your dreams and become an above-average individual. It is as simple as that.

Waiting for the "right opportunity" is much like waiting for God. You might not realize the right opportunity has come and gone if you are blind to it, even if it is right in front of you or in you, but you are too blind to see it or feel it.

It is important to understand that creating an opportunity is often better than waiting for the right one. You need to realize there is a degree of uncertainty which needs to be faced when going into anything considered worthwhile. Do you focus on the uncertainty or on the endless possibilities that await you when you take the first step to a life of purpose with meaning? It is all up to you.

In my experience in business, I have seen many missed opportunities to create value for shareholders. Unfortunately, there are those who want all of the information before making a decision, while there are others who find it acceptable to make a decision using only 80% of the information; that is, the 80% they believe contains sufficient and appropriate information to do so, leaving the remaining 20% of uncertainty as their level of risk tolerance. Usually, people in the latter category never use the excuse that they are waiting for the right opportunity as they either create the right opportunity or use 80% of the information and opportunity to proceed with a business decision. The same can be said for life's opportunities, and that is to embrace opportunities as they come, even when uncertainty exists. I am not saying that all opportunities should be embraced, but that all should be considered and not discounted immediately due to a lack of certain, often unnecessary, and unimportant information. There is a saying to trust your gut. I have found that many people end up saying, "I wish I had…" Don't let that be you. Life lessons include taking calculated chances, so don't use the excuse that you are waiting for the right opportunity to let life's lessons pass you by.

There is another extreme on the spectrum with regard to this mindset as well. For example, changing directions with every perceived opportunity and being too fast and loose when it comes to risk. You should not be piling all your eggs into one basket, as the saying goes, hoping for the best and taking risks when the rewards are not worth it.

Risks need to be taken when you understand that you stand to gain something of significant worth. There is a big difference between investing in a stock and buying a lotto ticket - one is a leap of uncertainty, and the other is a jump into the void. You need to be smart about the opportunities you take and the ones you create, but do not ignore them if they do not look "right" at first glance or if they seem like too much work for the expected and potential return.

Nothing of worth can be achieved if there is no uncertainty, risk, or work involved. Do not wait for the right opportunity to start following your dreams. Waiting for the perfect opportunity is nothing but a delaying tactic for the weak-willed and the risk-averse. It is the kind of "safe" life which might not be worth living at all when you really think about it.

The next time you find yourself waiting for "the right opportunity" to pursue your dreams, think about the future when you are on your deathbed. Imagine asking yourself - was it worth not taking advantage of the opportunity when it came knocking at your door? What would have happened if only you had stepped forward, taken the risk, and it resulted in a lifetime of fulfillment? You will never know unless you step in faith and grab hold of the opportunities before you if you only believe the rewards will be worth it.

The choice is yours!

5

"LIFE'S NOT FAIR"

"It's not fair, it never was, it isn't now, it won't ever be. Do not fall into the entitlement trap of feeling you are a victim, you are not. **Get over it and get on with it.** *And yes, most things are more rewarding when you break a sweat to get em."*
~ Matthew McConaughey

Surprise! The excuse "life's not fair" is the catch-all for every excuse we have dealt with so far, as well as those we will deal with later in this book.

At 21 months old, my son was diagnosed with a rare form of cancer called 'bilateral retinoblastoma.'

It was then, for the first time since I was a boy, that I cried. Imagine the words, "your son has cancer." I thought that life was just not fair for a toddler to have cancer, and I cannot tell you how much that really tested my faith in God. Why would God allow for my son, or any child, to have cancer? What kind of God would allow that to happen? Then it hit me that I was doing myself no favors in complaining or making excuses for what had occurred, as the real test was how my wife and I would handle this challenge.

When my son was diagnosed with cancer, I had every reason to yell at God for being unfair, and in my darkest moments, I did. But yelling at the Universe gets you nowhere…fast. A year after my son's cancer diagnosis, he was diagnosed with autism. Again, another reason to give up, to throw in the towel and complain about life not being fair; another opportunity to yell at the void. It took every fiber of my being to reconcile my faith with the unfairness of life. It also made me much less concerned and not likely to be receptive to those who complained that life was not fair as they did not have Wi-Fi or internet service at their cottage. The point here is that life is indeed not fair, but using it as an excuse does nothing to advance the achievement of your goals and the joy of living a life of purpose with meaning, even in the most difficult of situations and circumstances.

Life's not fair…compared to what? Is basketball fair? Is being sick fair? Is death and destruction fair? Is crime fair? What about the 100 M sprint? How about university? Of course they are all not fair, but they exist. In basketball, you have to be a certain height, or the deck is stacked against you. If you do not have enough money or access to loans to help with tuition, you end up feeling screwed; believe me, the cost of university does not seem fair, either. Think about your favorite heroes. Was life fair to them? Life is not fair…but that is not an excuse to not live a life of purpose with meaning.

It is because life was not fair to Mike Tyson that he grew up to be a killer in the ring. The unfairness of life often produces diamonds, and that is why complaining about the unfairness of life is so dangerous to our success. Whether we like it or not, the unfairness of life can bring out the best or worst in us, but ultimately, we have a choice. Experience is often the best teacher, and the worst experiences invariably teach us the best lessons if we choose to look at each experience that way. We are not truly equal when we come into this world; at least not when it comes to our circumstances. Some people are born with the proverbial silver spoon in their mouths, whilst some are utterly alone and without any support structure at all. Life is not fair. It is one of the first truths a child learns about the real world. We are not all dealt the same hand in this world, but almost everyone should understand that their lot in life is under their control and can be changed as they grow up. While it is quite true that life is not fair, it is also obvious that we need to learn to deal with that fact. We must teach ourselves to work around life's unfairness rather than giving up and refusing to fight for our dreams and passion.

Way too many people lose all hope when their mentality becomes too nihilistic and negative, thinking that because life is not fair, then perhaps it is not worth living at all. These people often experience despair and hopelessness, fall into depression, and some even reach the point of committing suicide because the negativity overwhelms them.

Everyone has unique challenges which need to be faced and overpowered. Each of us has distinct journeys we must go through to get where we want and need to be in our lives.

You need to understand that even though life is quite unfair, you have both freewill and time, which can be used to achieve near-impossible things with courage and determination. Whether it be in financial terms, in natural talent, or sheer luck, one person may be more gifted than another, but often, hard work, pure desire, and will can give a less-gifted individual the upper hand.

When the odds are against you, it does not mean you do not have a chance to find success—it just means you may have to work harder to achieve your dreams. Innovation, creativity, and adaptability are core traits within you, and you can use these powerful traits as a leveler to even the playing field.

There are several excellent examples of successful people who have overcome great odds to get where they wanted to be in life. One of the most impactful examples is a child who could not speak for the first three years of his life. His development was so delayed that his teachers often commented on his apparent laziness and low IQ. Yet, this child came up with one of the most impactful theories in the scientific realm: the theory of relativity. We all know him as none other than Albert Einstein—a name synonymous with genius in the modern age. Another child dropped out of school at the age of fifteen when his family became homeless and was forced to live in a van. We know him today as Jim Carrey, who has gained worldwide fame and is synonymous with comedic acting in the modern era. In each instance, these individuals were born with a gift, which they ultimately uncovered later in life. In adulthood, they honed those gifts and transformed their lives into the masterpieces they were meant to be and dominated their respective fields for generations.

Early life was certainly not fair to them. They faced the challenges and worked around them, playing the hand life had dealt them. They used their gifts, applying their strong will, hard work, and perseverance to achieve greatness. It is a model we would do well to follow.

Thomas Edison failed at creating a functioning light bulb ten thousand times before he achieved the single success which changed the course of history.

Clearly, it does not really matter whether or not life is fair, nor does it matter if some people have more opportunities than others. What truly matters and makes all the difference is what we do with what we are given, however large or small. It is a fact but, more importantly, an outlook which is more valid than the "life's not fair "ideology. Plus, it is an infinitely more beneficial mindset to cultivate. Looking at the problems we face in this way allows us to tap into adaptability, problem-solving, and creative thinking capabilities which are not otherwise possible, particularly when we constantly lament that life is not fair and use the mantra as an excuse not to do anything. Doing so is just another way of redirecting blame and convincing ourselves that it is not our fault if we have not pursued our dreams.

With this mindset, you come to believe that the unfairness of life is part and parcel of the deal. In truth, life will throw challenges at you, and the more you try to achieve greatness, the more difficult these challenges will get. The key is to remain steadfast in the face of such challenges, look for ways to overcome these obstacles, and pursue your dreams - come what may.

We must simply accept the fact that inherent unfairness exists and so it must be factored into our overall plan and faced without complaint. Overcoming these unfair situations, circumstances, and challenges makes life worth living. It is why everyone loves an underdog story - victory triumphs despite the odds and is so much more gratifying and sweeter than an easy win.

People who look at life through a more positive lens despite life's unfairness, seeking to solve problems equitably, nearly always find themselves prospering. Conversely, people who view life through the lens of negativity find themselves falling behind in all aspects of life. Such a lens of weakness, insecurity, fear, and doubt only leads to inaction, while a lens of strength, hope, and joy has the opposite effect.

At some point in our lives, we all have thoughts about how unfair life is, but those thoughts should last only for a while, long enough for us to gather our strength and overcome them. When our focus is on our goals and fulfilling our purpose in life, there is no time to use "life is not fair" as an excuse. The choice to face the basic truth that life is not fair will determine whether or not you can live a life of purpose or one of abject defeat and misery.

The choice is yours!

6

"I CAN'T WORK WITH LOSERS"

Before I delve into this excuse, I want to be perfectly clear that I am vehemently opposed to labeling of any kind.

I used to be one who, like many in society, generalized individuals by race, country of origin, political affiliations, family name, school alumni, group identities, religion, etc.

While many would deny using generalizations to identify individuals by their assumed personalities, we all have such biases and have used them in one way or another. Rather than deny having used these biases and stereotypical oversimplifications, we must come to realize that, on the surface, though there may seem to be some truth in many generalizations, they are almost always unfounded and invalid in describing the entire group. Next, we must consider how to change our thinking and double down on recognizing incorrect perceptions of others. I did it and so can you.

Today, I strive to see people as individuals and not make determinations about whom they are based on external classifications or group identities. Why? In traveling the world, I have met the humblest, most caring, generous, and selfless individuals from all races, ages, and religions. My personal experiences have led me to conclude that human beings, no matter how they were brought up, have a mind free to understand, observe, rationalize, and make decisions. We are born with free will to choose how to follow our passions, achieve our goals, serve others, and think of others as individuals based on their individual characteristics, personalities, and actions and not group identity.

To this end, I do not, under any circumstances, believe anyone should be called a "loser," as it is just an opinion based on bias rather than facts. If someone has made choices or continues to make choices which lead to failures, it does not make them a loser, even if, in fact, they have lost or continue to lose. My reason for saying this is that even winners have often lost several times before winning or beginning a winning streak. I would accept the loser description if society used it in context, but often it is used loosely and in a negative fashion, compared to doing so constructively. Alternatively, no one should be called a winner, without context, if their choices have led to success. Why? Consider those who have been called winners for their successes. In most instances, they have also had many failures, which means they were losers at some point. Even so, it is not okay to call someone a loser until they begin to win and succeed, as where does one draw the line? Does one go in and out of being a winner and a loser as life's failures and successes occur? Thinking so seems quite shallow, short-sighted, and negative.

The underlying philosophy here may seem quite subtle, but it is significant. My philosophy is that people are not winners in and of themselves, as some have, at times in their lives, failed or made losing decisions.

I propose that those we call winners possess a winning attitude and mindset. Similarly, those who continuously lose or fail have a losing mindset. Calling someone a winner or loser is too definitive and finite when the same person can move between being a winner and a loser and vice versa. The overriding thought here is that choosing to have a winning mindset or a losing mindset continuously invariably evolves into a habit which is normally sustained. The choice of which mindset we choose is all up to each individual, as, let's be clear, it is a choice.

Going forward, let's see people who continue to win as having a winning mindset and those who continue to lose as having a losing mindset. The choice is ours. The key is such words are simply words which allow others to assess their thinking, focusing on the freedom of their mind to choose the attitude which can then develop into a habit on a pathway to success. It is a much better approach than calling someone a loser, as doing so is negative and helps no one on their journey of self- discovery.

Notice I did not say one should sugarcoat the reality in another person's life. In our thoughts and our speech, we should strive to be the light that shines as an example to others versus the darkness that fuels depression, lack of drive, low self-esteem, and low self-worth, which are so prevalent in many people in the world today. With a new understanding of my personal philosophy regarding name-calling, let's now debunk the excuse "I can't work with losers." We already know those who use this excuse need to stop doing so immediately so they can take the next step towards a life of purpose with meaning. But how?

We've heard it before and maybe even said it ourselves—"I can't work with losers." It is one of the worst possible excuses. The only real factor which can stop you from achieving greatness is you. Everything else, all the other excuses, are just that—excuses.

When people say I can't work with losers, they combine two serpents in one: the serpent of excuses and the serpent of complaints. The combination of excuses and complaints is a deadly one.

"I can't work with losers" is something you hear a lot from certain people these days. For example, when leaders say that they can't work with losers, what they really mean is that they don't know how to motivate their team or collaboratively work with others. For managers and leaders, the inability to motivate a team hurts, and it is a pain that every manager experiences on their way to the C-suite, with some never really overcoming this challenge. The challenge of motivation is real, and it is difficult. However, we do not make challenges easier by lying to ourselves.

I can't work with losers is a lie, and we are not going to lie to ourselves anymore. Every leader is primarily a motivator, and motivating people who are not currently excited about their job is the primary role of every strong leader. Similarly, working with colleagues who do not pull their weight can be extremely frustrating, but using that as an excuse for one's own incompetence is futile and leads to nowhere. It is not to motivate or force people to do what they do not want to do but to motivate and inspire them to believe they can do what they otherwise would never have thought possible.

Ubuntu. It is a Swahili word that stands for "I am because we are. We are all one." And it is a tough pill to swallow for managers who blame their team for their failure. I am because we are. If you think your team member is a loser, then what does that say about you?

One of the unhealthiest excuses of all time is to blame the people around you for "holding you back." It is an unacceptable excuse, and quite a pathetic one if you truly believe another person or the perceived lack of any skill, talent, or drive is the reason you are not able to achieve your dreams.

This mentality is too pervasive in our society and needs to be challenged as well as changed going forward. In the past, I would have said there are too many sheep in this world and not enough shepherds; that is, there are too many followers and not enough leaders. However, not everyone can or should be a leader– after all, if all of us were leaders, whom would we be leading?

The key is to believe in yourself and to focus on your talents, skills, and gifts, using them in the service of others. Too many people try to change others rather than changing themselves. I used to be one who looked at my relatives and friends and could not understand why they were not using the gifts and skills that they had to be phenomenal success stories. It took years before I began to look within. I realized it was futile, and the greatest change I could make was to unleash the power from within me and use my skills more than I had ever done before.

If only we would look into our souls and uncover the power from within to serve others, there would be nothing we could not achieve. Instead, we look to external factors, like the accomplishments or lack thereof in others, to determine our destiny or use them as the excuse for why we cannot be better versions of ourselves. No one, when confronting themselves in the proverbial mirror, can reasonably arrive at any other conclusion than this behavior, and these excuses are without merit.

People who have purpose and seek to achieve that purpose inevitably end up being successful in life. They are seen as beacons of hope and signals of possibility for others to follow. No one wants to emulate a person who constantly complains or uses excuses to avoid taking the first step toward a life of purpose with meaning. Successful people aren't necessarily wealthy people, but rather those who have set goals for themselves and strive to accomplish them every time. They do not sit around and wait for life to happen, but work to make things happen in an active manner.

If you are not pursuing your passion and aren't trying to get ahead in life because of the lack of "winners "around you, then you will always be considered a "loser," even if you are not. Remember that I define the term loser as a person with a losing mindset, since no one is a loser for life unless they choose to continue having a losing mindset. It is a hard truth to accept, but failure can be overcome when adopting a winning mindset.

The "loser" label may not seem so important when you are using it to describe others. Yet, it is extremely dangerous, as well as unfortunate, when individuals act in a way which essentially labels them, consciously or not, as losers. Choosing a winning mindset brings success, while choosing a losing mindset often continues to result in failure. Both are completely dependent on the individual in question—not someone else.

There are multiple issues with the "I can't work with losers" excuse, and every single one holds you back from achieving greatness. First, the lack of a winning team can be attributed to multiple factors. Let's begin with those issues that reflect why and how they hold you back and the ways to successfully escape the conundrum they present.

Anyone who says they "can't work with losers" can only say so truthfully if they are working hard on their own and the only factor holding them back is the people with whom they have surrounded themselves. Otherwise, they are just making another excuse, much like "I am waiting for the right opportunity" excuse. At the root of it, this excuse is simply a way of shifting blame from one's own lack of self-will or ingenuity onto the supposed weaknesses of others.

If you think this way, you need to realize that the lack of a winning "team" can be attributed to you and you alone. People seldom flock around those who do not put in the hard work themselves. The "I can't work with losers" excuse is often used by bosses and other workplace leaders who like taking ownership of successes and dispersing all the blame when plans fall short. Doing so leads to a drop in morale across the entire team, which results in the deterioration of the workplace environment, causing a downward spiral which often ends in ruin.

Many people have experienced this phenomenon on the job, while volunteering, or even in a classroom. When no one is willing to take ownership of the project/work, nothing ever gets done and everyone points fingers at each other for the lack of results.

Negative and defeatist thoughts also manifest when there is a genuine case of circumstances making it difficult, but not impossible, to put together a winning team.

If you deem your circumstances difficult but possible, you are free to consider all the options, potential solutions, and a successful path forward by never giving up or losing hope. The keyword used in the sentence is "possible," not "impossible." Your dreams and your purpose are too important to allow you to fall by the wayside due to difficult circumstances.

If you find yourself surrounded by the so-called "losers," then the onus is on you to change it. Success and opportunity do not fall into the laps of those who use petty excuses to sit back and do nothing.

"Winners" are people who have skills or put forth the effort to acquire the skills necessary to accomplish their goals. They tend to gravitate towards similar individuals (go-getters) who do not allow circumstances like their environment and the people around them to hold them back.

It is exactly what you need to do as well, especially if you keep saying the reason you cannot pursue your passions or a meaningful, joyful life is because you are being held back by the people around you. Learn to let go and move forward. Letting go begins in the mind and invariably results in a different way of speaking, leading to actions that can only lead to success and the achievement of your goals.

If your friends have interests that are not productive or they use excuses to avoid changing their circumstances, it would be in your best interest to try to convince them to improve their ways or move on. While it may seem difficult to do, if you don't, you have only yourself to blame. You can't blame anyone else if you choose to remain in the current situation with no path forward and no goal or plan. It is always up to you to make any change needed in your life to move forward and strive for success.

It can be even more challenging if the people holding you back are your family, but the same holds true in this case as well. If your family members are "holding you back" due to their mindset and what they say to you, then you need to establish a distance between yourself and them or cut them off so you can pursue your dreams. To be clear, this does not necessarily mean you need to physically get away from them, but if you have to do so to move forward, then it is what you need to do. In doing so, it may not only be best for you but for them as well.

I have seen many people decide on such a path, become successful beyond their means, and support their families in ways they never dreamed of doing. They would never have been able to do so had they remained in their self-imposed prison, perpetrated by thoughts of how their family members held them back, only to realize late in life that the only person holding them back was themselves.

An alternative and meaningful approach is to have a positive mindset so focused that family members' words and actions cannot impact your achieving your goals. It is here that you become a new creation by uncovering the real you and the power within, and recognizing that while you belong to a family, you are not defined by your family. You realize the greatest masterpiece of creation is you, and you deserve to unleash the power from within, despite any negative influences around you. If you cannot distance negative influences from your mind, you need to put these individuals out of your life, so you can attract people with more positive mentalities who are focused on self-discovery and not excuses. There is a famous saying which declares that a person is defined by the company he or she keeps. Equally true is the fact that the person is responsible for the kind of company they keep.

The truth of the matter is, these types of excuses are used because we become comfortable with mediocrity and no longer wish to escape the mire in which we find ourselves. In most cases, the excuse is not even applicable because most people who use these excuses have cultivated their friend groups and thus cannot blame anyone else for their own failings and shortcomings.

There are so many examples of individuals who have come from backgrounds which are not considered conducive to success. Yet, they have been able to pull themselves up by their bootstraps and find co-workers and friends to come alongside and achieve success. Even more so, there are those who have been able to move from neighborhoods, towns, cities, and even countries to pursue their dreams and find fertile ground in which to grow and achieve success, living a life of purpose with meaning.

An incredibly understated example is the amazing case of Ursula Burns, the former CEO of Xerox. Ursula's parents immigrated to the United States from Panama. She grew up in a housing project in New York and later started as an intern at Xerox. Burns climbed the ranks and achieved greatness, becoming the CEO of a Fortune 500 company and being named number 22 on Fortune's list of the most powerful women in the world.

Burns checks all the boxes of underprivileged individuals: female, Black, daughter of immigrants, grew up in the projects. She did not lament the lack of privilege and opportunity or blame the "losers" around her. Instead, she worked hard from the ground up and was thus able to attract the winning team she needed to find her success working for one of the biggest companies in the world at that time. If Burns was able to encounter and overcome so many factors which would be described as bad hands, then we can have absolutely no excuse. Having "losers" around you is not conducive to success, but keeping them around, mentally or physically, and using them as an excuse is a choice you make.

If you are determined to grow beyond them, you will need to harness your own skills, ingenuity, and hard work to attract similarly minded individuals who can help you achieve your life's goals. If your circumstances do not allow it, then you must learn to let go of the people who hold you back and find those who will help you flourish.

When you are driven and understand what needs to be done to achieve an end goal, people—the right kind of people—will be attracted to you. These individuals are very important to have in your life for long-term success because they serve as anchors for you to stabilize yourself when situations and circumstances get tough. The only way to get "winners" to come into your life is to become like them, providing drive, integrity, and character, which they will value in you as much as you value those traits in others.

The key is to become active and pursue your dreams the right way, without labeling anyone or using others as a reason to be passive and allow things to happen to you. I don't like saying the word, but if you use the excuse that you can't work with losers, in the end, the only loser ends up being you. The choice is yours!

7

"I'M NOT READY"

"The world isn't changed by people who are ready."
- Richie Norton

When I hear someone say "I am not ready" as an excuse, the example of the Israelites from the Old Testament comes to mind. They always seemed to lack the will to take the necessary action.

The Israelites were easily "swayed by the wind," going whichever way it blew as situations and circumstances changed. They always did so to their own detriment. They allowed things to happen to them, and no matter what occurred, they did not lift a finger of their own volition to save themselves.

They cried out to God to free them from slavery in Egypt, but once God set the wheels of change in motion and the going got tough, they decided they weren't ready and wanted to head back to the way it was in Egypt. These people held God responsible for their situation, asked God for help, and when they got what they were asking for, they said they were not ready.

They also became impatient as they looked to external factors to define themselves, as evidenced by having Moses's brother, Aaron, make an idol for them in the form of a golden calf when Moses was gone too long from them.

They could not be patient as they were told to be. They were so dependent on others to provide for them that they had to replace their faith with something that was immediate to them in the form of an idol. They were not ready for the change they received.

The following verses are from Proverbs, making the point that waiting for the time when you are ready to make a positive change will end up leaving you in a worse position than when you began.

"I passed by the field of a sluggard, by the vineyard of a man lacking sense, and behold, it was all overgrown with thorns; the ground was covered with nettles, and its stone wall was broken down. Then I saw and considered it; I looked and received instruction. A little sleep, a little slumber, a little folding of the hands to rest, and poverty will come upon you like a robber, and want like an armed man." (Proverbs 24:30-34)

The fact is that the "sluggard" is the one with a defeatist mindset, and this verse from the Bible is for those that have this mindset; therefore, I challenge each one to do whatever it takes to change this mindset to become better versions of themselves each day.

The next time you find yourself saying that you are not ready, remember that the bad times and poverty can "come upon you like a robber, and want like an armed man."

Having spent a considerable time thinking about this particular excuse, I was able to get over my initial judgment response towards the people that use it.

I began to understand why people say that they are "not ready" when asked why they have not taken the necessary steps to accomplish their dreams—the people that talk about their dreams; some plan and some do not, but many end up not doing anything at all.

The "I'm not ready" excuse is founded primarily on fear and doubt. They would rather live in the comfort of the 'known' versus the perceived dark streets of the 'unknown'. The "readiness" being referred to is not a physical thing but a mental hold-up that many have, preventing them from accomplishing anything worthwhile in their lives, becoming resentful and depressed in their supposed "golden years." The essence of this excuse is nothing but fear.

Think about it—stepping out into the unknown can seem scary. It is much easier to use the excuse "I'm not ready" and stay where you are—comfortable in the familiar. So, the first part of the fear that fuels this excuse is the fear of the unknown and the fear of leaving the comfort zone that becomes a cage that prevents us from reaching or unleashing our potential.

This is the same reason why the Israelites wanted to turn back when things got tough, wanting the familiarity of oppression rather than the freedom that came with unfamiliar strife.

Freedom was simply out of their comfort zone, and they looked to outside sources to help them.

When they felt like they did not have that, when Moses was absent, they quickly replaced their own faith with a false idol. So fickle were they, and so without purpose, that they could not do anything to change their circumstances. Even after being freed from slavery in Egypt, they continued to feel themselves as not being 'ready' for freedom; can you imagine? So many people have not learned the lesson that the true power is within us and not in anything external—there is no fairy that will arrive in the night and sprinkle us with some magic dust that will make us "ready" for what we need to do.

Whether one believes in God or not, we are each made perfect in our own way. Sadly, many do not realize this incredibly important fact. God has already given us the tools we need to be "ready" to follow the path required to fulfill our purpose. God has already blessed us with life, with time, and with the potential to achieve our dreams. We do not understand that we are already "ready" to do what needs to be done, or at least we are ready to take the steps required to learn, to nurture, to harness the skills and talents we have in order to live a life of purpose with meaning, and without using excuses.

When I consider the Israelites, even for only a few moments, I realize I have never been like them. Thankfully, I am different in the way I think, not falling into the same traps that they did. As a child, it did not seem that there was an option to disobey my parents or God in such drastic and perverted ways as the Israelites did.

I never saw the need to conform to what the others at my schools did. I simply refused to be "swayed by the wind" in my endeavors. However, I admit that I did not always see my purpose so clearly or embrace the power from within as I should have. I am now clear in my understanding of my purpose, which has led me to the kind of contentment and absolute joy that I wish others to have—the very reason I am writing this book in the first place.

From a very young age, my parents taught me that I needed to think for myself and choose to do what was right. I have always sought to do so and hope I have done so more often than not.

I have occasionally had differences of opinion with my family as well as my parents, but none were similar in nature to the Israelites who lacked the will to take action, changed their minds with the wind, were impatient, and often sought to focus on idols.

Once again, I'll say, excuses are just that—excuses. I'll even dare to say all excuses come from a single source–the desire to remain in one's comfort zone, also known as the fear of the unknown, or, to be exact, the fear of unknown perceived discomfort. Many people would rather stay in their mediocre jobs, earning less and being miserable, or not pursue their dreams and live an unfulfilled life than go through the joy and suffering that is involved with taking the risk of using their skills and talents to live a purpose-driven life.

In this way, many are much like the Israelites who wanted to return to Egypt and have a life of bondage when the going got tough. "I'm not ready" is simply an excuse to remain in our comfort zone, fearful of what might happen if we take the risk and step into the unknown.

I have established that this is not a valid excuse, as no excuse is; it should not hold you back.

The joy and suffering involved with jumping into the unknown in the effort to achieve your dreams is much sweeter than the safety of a mediocre existence and having regrets for the rest of your life.

But how do we get over this hang-up? What should you think about the next time you tell yourself, or others, that you are "not ready" to live your purpose? Well, we can go back to the example of the Israelites; specifically, Moses, the leader of the Israelites.

Moses was also not ready, even as the one chosen by God to lead the Israelites out of Egypt. Moses questioned God as to why he would be able to convince Pharaoh to let the Israelites go or how he could lead them out of Egypt.

"Come now therefore, and I will send thee unto Pharaoh, that thou mayest bring forth my people the children of Israel out of Egypt. And Moses said unto God, who am I, that I should go unto Pharaoh, and that I should bring forth the children of Israel out of Egypt?" (Exodus 3:10-11)

He was not ready for his role, and he did not have complete information on what to do. He had a goal, and he worked towards it-come what may.

The truth is that no one is ready, not leaders, not great men, and women, but what differentiates great men and women from those that cannot do what needs to be done is that they take action whether they are ready or not.

Moses did what had to be done only because his faith allowed him to step out and do it, instead of using the excuse that he was not ready.

It should be no surprise to hear my response to the one using the "I'm not ready" excuse every day, every week, every month, every year, is that in all likelihood, if they believe they are not ready, they likely will never be ready.

How do we deal with people who think that they are "not ready" and cannot bring themselves to work to achieve their dreams and follow their purpose?

We need to talk to them, encourage them, and try and dispel the notion that anyone needs to be a hundred percent ready to start working towards their dreams.

While this may seem negative, challenging someone's thinking to the actual reasons they believe they are not ready is healthy.

Even if you agree that they are not ready today, it does not mean that they cannot be ready tomorrow or the day after. The issue is really those who constantly use the excuse without doing anything to "'be ready". It is then you can encourage them to try anyway. That is how most successful people do it—by not waiting to be perfectly ready to do what needs to be done. The fact of the matter is that we humans are not islands separated from others; we are very much affected by the words and actions of others if we choose to be. You can be the reason why someone else is able to follow their passions and find purpose in life.

Many people would not have succeeded in life were it not for the support and encouragement of others and their assistance in helping to remove fear and doubt, or to boldly act, despite fear and doubt, as this is where courage is vital to one's success. These are the kinds of friends you want and need close to you rather than those who never give you encouragement to follow your dreams and confirm your fears rather than dispel them.

Have you ever heard someone accepting an award give thanks to the people in their lives who made a significant contribution to their achievement and success? Of course, we all have.

People often say, "if it were not for a specific person who repeatedly told me that I 'could' when I thought I 'could not,'" or they give thanks to the person who encouraged them to continue when they wanted to give up.

We have also heard many who reminded everyone of the ones who told them they would not amount to anything, but they did anyway. Amazing how having the right mindset makes all the difference in our life's journey.

It is a balance one must reach, garnering support as needed from those with a positive, encouraging mindset. In fact, I believe that one should never proceed with anything, even if one believes that he or she is not ready, if one has a negative mindset. Much success has been gained by those who thought that they were not ready but had a positive mindset and moved ahead anyway.

They either felt they had nothing to lose or were willing to take the risk. They believed that the risk of not being ready was worth it to at least venture into the unknown and take a chance at success.

If you have this mindset, then you will not have to live with regrets of not having tried. If you think you are not ready, do not wait for when you will be ready because the truth is that you might never really be ready at all.

"I'm not ready" should never be an excuse for not fulfilling your purpose and achieving your goals in your life. Such an excuse should not prevent you from sharing life's precious moments with the ones you love, doing the things you are passionate about, taking risks to pursue your goals, and not living with regret in mediocrity.

Many will say, "You will know you are ready when God sends you a sign."

While that may be true, sadly, such signs come and go frequently as most lay passively, hoping for a burning bush or some equally elaborate miracle to happen.

"Don't be afraid. Just stand still and watch the Lord rescue you today. The Egyptians you see today will never be seen again. The Lord himself will fight for you. Just stay calm." Then the Lord said to Moses, "Why are you crying out to me? Tell the people to get moving!" (Exodus 14:13-15)

Even God told Moses to not wait for help, to get on with it and tell the people to get moving. The truth is, such signs and miracles are often in the form of small incidents and experiences, which go unnoticed because people are waiting for God to visit them with a blinding light or a thunderous voice instead of realizing God's presence is within them all along.

Executing on the actions which use your gifts and talents will always prove rewarding beyond your wildest dreams, so enough with the excuses—choose to be ready and make things happen in your life.

God is not coming to save you, give you a sign, or do it for you, as God has already blessed you with life and your unique talents. You were created in God's image and have all you need to live a fulfilling and abundant life. God's greatest creation and masterpiece is YOU! YOU ARE READY!

The choice is yours!

E = mc²
E = mc²
E = mc²

8

"PEOPLE JUST DON'T UNDERSTAND ME"

"Don't try to explain yourself to people. If they don't get you, they don't get you. Simple"

What does the excuse "people just don't understand me" actually mean? I am perplexed - why would anyone care whether others understand them or not if they are being themselves? We live in a world where so many people are so insecure, they hang on to every word others say; they look for acceptance in every social media post; they seek approval in every physical encounter. Who cares whether people understand you or not?

This is an excuse you often hear from certain people, even those that possess brilliance that others admire. Their brilliance dims their empathy. And without empathy, their brilliant ideas die with them. So, when people don't understand you, whose fault is it? "People just don't understand me" is extremely powerful, and it's powerful because it's an excuse that feeds your confidence.

When you say, "People just don't understand me," what you're really claiming is that they're not smart enough to understand you. You're blaming the student for misunderstanding the lesson, rather than criticizing the mess you wrote on the chalkboard.

People enjoy making this excuse, and it comes in many variations:

- "What they don't understand is…"
- "What they fail to realize is…"
- "What they're forgetting is…"

Do you see how deflective these statements are? These statements are never focused on ourselves, as it is always the other person who has the problem.

Having people understand what you say is crucial to being an effective communicator and sustaining relationships, both personally and professionally, so it is not the focus of this excuse. The "people don't understand me" excuse is more descriptive of a person with behaviors that do not align with those around them. In such cases, unless they are harming themselves or hurting others, the question should be, "Does anyone have to understand, in full or in part, others?" Did everyone have to understand Einstein and his peculiar behaviors and interests, or did they just need to respect his genius? Did anyone have to understand Thomas Alva Edison's genius and the fact he tested the light bulb over 10,000 times before it actually worked? Surely, few at that time, and without hindsight, would have understood why he did not give up much earlier.

Invariably, the issue is using the excuse "people just don't understand me" limits your progress, often causing you to curl up in a shell and never live your life of purpose. It is the very flaw you need to remove.

We must find our purpose in serving others with the gifts and talents we have. By living our lives with meaning and a sustaining joy, we remove any time and effort we were using to consider whether people understand us or not. Why? The preoccupation with living a life of purpose is so fulfilling there is no time to wonder whether others like us or dislike what we say or do. Living such a life is one free from hate, focused on ourselves and our purpose, leaving no room for anything else! This may seem to come out of left field, but consider RuPaul, who is arguably the most commercially successful and well-known drag queen in the world. I recall seeing him on television in the 90s. What stood out to me, way back then, was his confidence. He in no way used the excuse "'no one understands me' so I will remain in my shell and not express myself the way I want, with passion and purpose." At least if he did ever have such an attitude, it was never reflected in his performances and his successes. It saddens me how so many others could not do the same and take a page from RuPaul's life book. It was not easy, but he persevered.

The world would be in a much better place were most people not taught to find happiness in the acceptance of others. In addition, there is almost no risk when we are taught to accept our purpose in life is to serve others and to do so with the gifts and talents we have, and to do so with a passion and fulfillment which cannot be denied.

The day a child or any adult human recognizes this truth is the day they are no longer focused on having others understand them so they can make life's important decisions. Life is too short to depend on the approval of others for life decisions. However, I often do not guarantee anything, but in this instance, I will make an exception and guarantee that there are those who will not understand you, but many will understand you as you pursue a meaningful life of purpose. I promise there is much in the world to do which would prove fulfilling if we can move our focus from wondering if others understand us and experience the inward joy of doing what we love in service to others.

The choice is yours!

9

"I'M TOO BUSY"

"Many people are busy, but doing what? Unless you are busy living a meaningful life by doing what matters in fulfilling your purpose, you should consider what you are busy doing."

No, often when this excuse is used, it really means that the person is afraid. Remember, fear and doubt are the reasons for excuses. When people say, "I'm too busy" what they are really saying is that they are afraid of doing what they are supposed to do.

We often get quite busy when we are afraid because it makes us feel good to be distracted. It gives us a temporary escape, at least to others, from the reality of the fact that we are afraid. Somehow, it makes us feel productive. It makes us feel like we are moving forward, but not all movement is progress. Instead of giving up on our dreams—which would be too painful to admit—we say, "we are too busy" to do what we wish we had the courage to do. Then, when someone implements our idea, we get to hold on to our status by telling our friends that we "predicted" or "thought of" the idea a long time ago. So when you say I'm too busy, it's a sign.

It's a sign that you are not doing what you are supposed to do. Luckily, it is also a sign that you are approaching the first obstacle in every hero's journey: Refusal of the Call. When people say they are too busy, what they are really saying is that they are afraid of continuing the hero's journey.

Have you ever wanted to just get things done and check off your never-ending to-do list? Have you ever procrastinated in taking the steps to do what you love or chasing dreams which would bring you fulfillment? Have you ever envied others for achievements that seemed simple to you?

Maybe you lamented, "That's easy, I can do that," or "I wish I could do that," or "I wish I had done that." All such statements have one thing in common—the 'lack of action'. Those statements are mere words. While you probably could do "it," whatever "it" is, we often take the easy way out in life. The fact is, no real success has ever been achieved by making excuses, not taking risks, and doing nothing. Many people in life find they are always busy, but sadly, most are busy performing tasks or engaging in activities they don't enjoy.

What's more worrying is that some do it because taking a risk would be too much trouble or carry too much uncertainty, so they keep the status quo, doing what they may be good at but not necessarily great at, and certainly not what they enjoy. Even worse are those who hate their jobs, their bosses, their co-workers, and their work but still stay, fearing they will not be able to get another job or earn a living in any other way.

Many even believe they would be unable to make a living at all if they follow their passion and try to fulfill their dreams. This is not the life we want to live, nor is it the life we were meant to have.

Now, I am not saying life is always a bed of roses, but life, as a journey, should be one where the journey is accomplished with purpose. If not, what use is life? Now, don't get the wrong idea. I am not saying you should just leave your job and jump into pursuing your purpose if your job is not aligned with such a pursuit. However, you should seek the path which leads to a life with meaning, so you may find the opportunity needed to leave your current job and step into your purpose, doing what you have the talents to do and doing so with a passion which can only come by doing what you love.

This may very well be staying in your current job, but working differently and more purposefully than ever before; you will be surprised what a difference this will make in your life, and I dare to say that others will see the transformation, too. No one has ever regretted doing what they love unless they have allowed external circumstances to derail them. It is often a case in which people are too busy to do what is meaningful because doing so would take them away from their comfort zones.

Why, then, should we complain when we do not have what we want or need in life? Why do we complain when we see others succeed, knowing we could do the same or better? Why? Why? Why? It is because looking outwardly at others is a way to cope. It also distracts us from looking in the mirror and asking the tough questions. For example, it might be someone who wants to change professions and has the means to do so, or it may be a person who wants to make a change, but there is some sacrifice they must make in order to succeed. In both situations, fear keeps them from taking action.

They often do not recognize they will either be in the same financial and personal situation if they don't succeed or be better off for stepping out in faith—even if the sacrifice seems insignificant or manageable.

In such a case, many engross themselves in work to artificially help them look and feel busy to avoid the following questions. Why? The answers may be too embarrassing to accept. The next time you find yourself making excuses of any kind, ask yourself the following five questions and answer honestly.

1. Will the change/action/effort kill or harm me in any way?
2. Will my decision and follow-through hurt others?
3. Will the action bankrupt me?
4. Will my family be hurt?
5. Will it destroy my soul?

If the answer is "no" to all the above questions, it may be time to take the risk and make the leap with the confidence that you will succeed. Being too busy is never a good excuse to avoid attempting to fulfill your dreams and find meaning in what you do.

Life's purpose calls for taking the necessary step and not busily spinning your wheels on a stationary bike, hoping you eventually get where you are meant to be.

The choice is yours!

10

"I DON'T HAVE ENOUGH MONEY"

"It pains me, somewhat, to see those who complain about not having enough money but are unwilling to make the sacrifices to earn the money they so desperately complain about not having."

Like most of the excuses in this book, "I don't have enough money" is often used by those who have always wanted to but never attempted to start a business aligned with what they love and in which they are proficient.

Behind this excuse is fear and doubt in their own abilities, plus the trepidation regarding whether anyone would pay to receive their service or product(s). Not having money is not the issue. I know too many people who continue to use this excuse—"You can't start a business without money."

While it is true, it is a poor mindset. Instead, consider this—it is not about whether you have the money, but whether you believe you can do what it takes to earn money, like being able to convince someone that your idea is worthwhile and you have the ability to manage such a business. Having an idea is easy, but managing the processes required to bring it to life may be difficult and challenging. Notice I did not say impossible, only difficult.

If you can't manage the processes, you need to find someone who can. Sadly, many owners are never willing to admit they can't run their own business. The mindset of the lack of money is the reason many give up before they start - they do not have the money they need to start their business. However, the problem is not about lacking the money but rather being able to see they can access the money needed if they step outside the box and do the hard work it takes to gain access to the required cash.

Here are a few ways a person who has insufficient cash to start a business can accomplish the goal:

1. Ask and you shall receive.
Most people are afraid to go to family and friends and ask for the funds needed. It is one thing to not have a clue as to what you want to do and ask for funds. It is a completely different scenario when you have a killer business plan and can knock on the doors of friends, family, or those who are in the industry and need your skills to take their business to the next level. Most people seem to go through life believing 100 percent of nothing is better than 50 percent of something.

With that type of thinking, you never entertain the fact that it may be more rewarding to ask for help, rather than doing it alone, often due to not wanting your great work or ideas to be stolen, manipulated, or copied.

However, how is that working out for you? Keeping your work a secret, yet complaining or making excuses as to why you are not living a better life, seems, and it is, a self-fulfilled prophesy and a self-inflicted wound that leads to nowhere but to an unfulfilled life.

Also, being afraid of rejection is one of the quickest ways to never achieve real success. The better option is to approach the people you know first and then seeking assistance or collaboration elsewhere. If you are uncomfortable approaching people you know, imagine how difficult it will be to approach a stranger, even with a killer business plan that shows the potential for significant profits.

2.   Prepare a household budget.

You need to make a choice to reduce your family's operating costs. You will be surprised how many people who claim they have "no money to start a business" drive expensive cars, pay exorbitant amounts of rent, eat out regularly, and the list goes on.

Are you one of them? Just imagine if you did a household budget and decided to cut back. In most cases, you would have more money to put down for a start-up than you imagined. Even if you didn't have enough, you would still look more favorable to friends, family, or investors; after all, who wants to invest in a start-up if, as the owner, you can't manage your personal spending and overall cash flow?

Sometimes, just the outward appearance sends the wrong message. For example, why would someone consider helping you as a would-be entrepreneur if you seem to be loose with your spending since it is very likely you would do the same with the business's funds? Sometimes downgrading your personal budget is the key to your success—on the journey to success, you may need to go down before you can go up. It all begins with setting a budget and sticking to it; no exceptions unless there is an emergency, an actual emergency, not one made up of an excuse.

3. Sacrifices must be made.

One such sacrifice is simply the need to take on more work. I say sacrifice because taking on a heavier workload means having to miss some important moments in your family's life or working twice as hard between these moments and never missing them.

The choice is always yours to make. Sadly, many people use not having enough money to sit around on their couch and watch Netflix every day instead of making the necessary sacrifices in the short term for greater gain in the long term. Many successful people have taken on two or more jobs to have enough cash to start a new enterprise.

Now, I believe this is the time to remind everyone that if you think you need $1 million to start your new business, then I would be curious to know what is your business. Many people believe they must have the best of everything from the start to deliver quality service or provide products people need, but the reverse is true.

After asking the tough questions, you realize it is all in your head and not based on facts but just the emotional connection of starting a business to be like the billion-dollar business which has been in existence for many years. You must be realistic but not limited in believing your business could grow into a billion-dollar business. There are no limits other than the ones you put on yourself, but your goals must be realistic.

No one should be able to convince you otherwise, as you will be doing whatever it takes to achieve your goals. Those who say "I have no money" as an excuse to start a business seldom make the sacrifices needed to accomplish their goals. I recently gave someone the above advice, and his response was, "I'm tired of being treated like I need to sacrifice more…I sacrificed enough to learn the skill and to survive this long."

You see how easy it is to lose your way and self-destruct? I had high hopes for this individual, but again, it brings me to the point—the decision to persevere and continue making the necessary sacrifices is up to you. Often, success is just around the corner, but too many people give up too early due to what they consider to be too many failed attempts.

4. Use social media to your advantage.

I can't tell you how many times I have advised people to get a social media presence in their field, especially if they are in an industry known to have millions of interests. Off the top of my head, a great example is being a cat lover. Let's say you have clothing for cats or a product or service people with cats would use.

The best way to get their attention is with lots of videos featuring your cat or cats with the products you sell or just highlighting your service(s) on a social media platform. You could call yourself "The Cat Lady XXX," and I guarantee it will be a winner. Why? The last time I checked, the most viewed YouTube videos were about cats.

Social media is not the end but can be the beginning. As someone who is so passionate about being a cat lover and has a related business, every time you are in public, you should highlight your services in some way. It shouldn't be hidden.

I know many people with such skills, though no one will ever know about their passion and the business they hope to get off the ground because they have no social media presence or any other significant connection with their potential customers.

5. For God's sake, launch a website.

You need a website, and you can have one for as little as $50 a month. You don't need all the bells and whistles, but should at least have a website to go with your YouTube presence. After all, when your target audience becomes bored with YouTube, you need a site where potential clients/customers can go to find out more about your business.

It pains me to see those who help friends with their websites but can't see their way clear to get their own website created and go live, using the excuse, "I have no money to start my business." Then there are others who eat out every day or every other day but can't set up a free website to start. Without a website, how are you going to be able to highlight the services and products you have to a wide target market? Word of mouth alone no longer cuts it, though it can help, as often word of mouth is facilitated by a social media presence.

To be able to spread the word about your business, you must strategically go out and make it happen. You must tell people and show them!

6. **Be bold and introduce yourself to like-minded individuals who may need your service or product.**

If you keep your great idea to yourself or are waiting on a brick-and-mortar store to introduce you to potential customers, you will be disappointed as most businesses require more work and effort than simply having a grand opening.

Many businesses in the 21st century do not need a physical presence—just an online presence. Even so, people need to know you exist. Be bold. Go out and make yourself and your services known. After all, what do you have to lose?

7. **YOU are the only one who knows your business intimately unless you are simply copying an existing business.**

If you are differentiating yourself from your competition, you are the only person who can convince someone you are the real deal. Fear of doing so needs to be overcome. I believe one way—the only way—to be prepared is to have a business plan. You've probably heard the adage, "If you fail to plan, you plan to fail." It is indeed true. I'm not saying you need to overthink planning, but it is essential to plan your path to success; at the very minimum, you need to have a basic plan from which to proceed.

Creating a business plan also prepares you to answer the tough questions others may ask. In fact, developing your business plan is essential and should be first on your list before you ask others to invest. It is a crucial step made more so for someone with no money. People who have money and no business plan can wing it and hope they are successful. They can even begin certain elements of their business in hopes of getting it right.

For those with no money, the luxury of hoping is nonexistent. Instead, there should be a thoughtful assessment of the risks, so you can convince friends, family, investors, or partners as to the viability, expected profitability, and reasonableness of the business. Telling someone to "trust me" is not the best or most effective way to gain access to cash.

The excuse of having no money is based on fear, doubt, and the unwillingness to do any or all of the above. Making excuses as to why you are not where you need to be is always because of the choices you make. I know many will disagree and blame every circumstance to justify that they had no choice, but I have shown people time and time again how this is not the case.

For example, let's say you need $10K to start a small business from your home. You say you don't have enough money, and so you have not been able to start the business. I ask, "How long have you been thinking about starting the business?" Let's say your response is three years. I then ask you to calculate how much you and your spouse could have saved in those three years if you had not eaten out every other day. It's $30/day, times 15 days a month, times 12 months, times three years.

Notice, I'm not including birthdays and special holidays like Christmas, where you generally spend more money between the two of you. Over a three-year period, the total is $16,200—$5,400 per year you could have saved in just meals. When I am finished with most people, the bottom line is that they could save a minimum of $5K/year for one person and a minimum of $12K/year for a couple. It is equally important to keep in mind how quickly one year goes by.

Granted, it requires discipline, which, if sought, removes the excuse of "I don't have enough money," but the question of

"WHY NOT?" remains. Your "why" is always surrounded by the choices you make. If you are not making enough money, the actions noted above should be acted upon and acted upon now.

The choice is yours!

pending
works
1 2 3
7 8 9

11

"I'LL DO IT TOMORROW"

"Let's face it: 'Tomorrow never comes', as how many tomorrows have you claimed in your lifetime?"

Ninety-nine percent of the time, "I'll do it tomorrow" is an often-repeated excuse made one day and the day after that, and the day after that, and so on.

It is likely one of the 'world's top five most used excuses. It is better known as procrastination, and no matter what culture or in what language, this excuse is used to delay doing what should be or what needs to be done.

Years ago, I said every time you use this excuse, if nothing has changed in your circumstances, then whatever the action intended, it must not have been important. Maybe you knew you needed to get a side job to increase your savings, but you offered the excuse "I'll do it tomorrow."

Each day, though you knew you needed to take action, something came up, and you repeated, "I'll do it tomorrow." At the end of a month or even a year, by how much could you have increased your savings? Instead, you actually lost money because of your poor excuse, "I'll do it tomorrow." Over the years, I have found this excuse to be among the weakest and one in which you have no one to blame but yourself.

"I'll do it tomorrow" is basically a delaying tactic, often elicited out of fear and doubt. If you say, "No, I'm not afraid or doubtful, I just haven't gotten to it yet," (an alternative iteration of "I'll do it tomorrow"), then you are likely employing the excuse because you lack focus or are unsure of what is truly important in your life. It all reminds me of one of Aesop's famous fables, "The Ants and the Grasshopper".

"All summer long, a merry grasshopper spent his days making music. When he saw the ants marching past him in a line, carrying seeds and grain to store in their hill, he laughed at their toil."

'How foolish, to work so hard in the hot sun!' the grasshopper said. 'Summer's the time to play and sing. There's time enough to worry about winter when the first snow falls.'

But when the days grew short, and the first snow fell, the grasshopper could find nothing to eat. Shivering in the cold, he came to ask the ants for help. 'Please, can't you spare me a seed or a leaf?' he begged. 'I'm too hungry even to sing!' The ants shrugged in disdain. 'We worked hard for our food, and we have none to spare,' they said. 'All summer long, you made nothing but music. Now all winter long, you dance!'

The moral of the story is, do not put off for tomorrow what you can and should do today. When tomorrow comes, there may be, and often are, many other things you need to do which can result in never actually doing what you should have done today. Have you ever seen someone working really hard to make their dreams come true? What did you say as you watched them working toward their goals? Maybe you sounded like the grasshopper and mocked their efforts, "How foolish, to work so hard!" And maybe, just maybe, when they succeeded, you had to come and ask them for help but conveniently forgot how you mocked them initially.

The "I'll do it tomorrow" excuse needs to be tossed out of your life just like every other excuse debunked in this book—it has no place in your life if you truly want to live a life of purpose and fulfillment.

The choice is yours!

I'm too old!
BUT ...
BUT ...
I'm not educated enough
BUT ...
I'm waiting for the right opportunity
I'm not ready
BUT ...
Life is not fair
BUT ...

12

"..., BUT..."

"Nothing productive ever comes from using the word 'but', as it often is followed by an excuse to explain away one's inaction."

But what? Have you ever had a desire to do something, but (this is the first and unfortunately not the last time you are going to see this word) fear and doubt got in the way?

Either via your thoughts and/or words or through your friends, family, or even strangers, you've heard the word "but" followed by an excuse.

Given the many excuses used each day by those with fear and doubt regarding achieving their goals, I am only going to present a few of the excuses using the word "but". It is important to understand that "but" is just another way of keeping yourself from living a life of purpose and doing what you know needs to be done or should be done.

"But" prevents you from living a meaningful life. Actually, it is not "but" which prevents you from living a meaningful life. Rather, and as painful as it may be to accept, it is YOU who is standing in the way of your success and keeping you from taking the next step to becoming a better version of yourself each day. Here are some examples of phrases using the word "but" followed by an excuse or excuses.

1. I would have done it, but I did not have enough money.
Can you imagine how debilitating it is to not only have such an excuse but also to have the audacity to use it? Not a single mention of what you did to get the money to do whatever it is you wanted to do.

Are you the only one on the planet who can't work towards the goal of getting the money to do what you need to do? I guess the sacrifices you would need to make are just too much to bear, so you just use the excuse instead of setting a goal, working out a plan, and striving to achieve the goals you set with reckless abandon.

It may mean the Mercedes Benz you are driving (and striving to make the payments so you can impress your friends) needs to be sold and replaced with a less costly vehicle or some other means of transportation to allow you to save more money toward your goal. Maybe the three-bedroom apartment or house you are working hard to pay the rent or mortgage for needs to be down-sized so you will have more money left toward your goal.

Is it possible you could stop eating at fast-food restaurants daily instead of preparing food at home and saving considerable money each day? I have provided financial advice to many, showing them how eating out daily for breakfast, lunch, and dinner, or even just lunch, can cost a person over $500 a month, which is over $6,000 a year.

Consider that you may have been doing this for years, yet you do not have $20,000 to start a home business. Remember, the $6,000 spent on fast-food restaurants and eating out each day, including weekends, is only a small part of the changes you could make to achieve your goals.

When included with rent, utilities, vehicle costs, entertainment, and other expenses, you might be surprised just how much could be saved towards your goals.

Don't forget, no one is tied to a low-paying job forever unless you choose to be, all stemming from having your incorrect mindset. My examples have all been about reducing cash outflow, but over time, it is all in the pursuit of ensuring your net cash inflow is positive and keeps growing. This can be accomplished whether it means making the changes I have noted, in addition to getting a different job, promotions, or starting a business, as examples.

In addition, it is not all about not having money but your ability to access the funds required to pursue your goals. If you had a revolutionary idea which would provide a much-needed service to many? Would you keep it to yourself or prepare a plan and walk the pavement, proposing it to anyone who would listen?

Many people tell me, "What if someone steals my plans?" My response is, "I can guarantee you no one would steal a plan that is hidden, but you can bet every penny you have that very few ideas are original, and sooner or later, someone else will come up with the plan on which you neglected to act."

You were born with a brain, so use it. You should never expose the secret sauce at a first meeting, or ever, unless it is lucrative to do so, but you should do whatever it takes to whet the appetite of the interested parties and investors. In short, like anyone who uses excuses, if you use the excuse of not having money and have no plan or strategy, you have only a pathetic excuse to not live the life you were meant to live. Please don't let this be you. The time is now to recognize your excuses, change your mindset, and believe you can, so you will.

2. I was going to start it, but other things got in the way.
This is likely one of the most used excuses, as it combines all the excuses one can find—from emergencies to the death of a loved one; from pregnancy to the loss of job; from the wrong place to the wrong time, etc.

Consider saying this excuse day after day, week after week, month after month, and year after year. After much time, it becomes a habit, and you eventually believe you can't as you have other things to do. As I mentioned before, I used to tell my daughter, "If you say you can't, then you can't. If you say you can, then you can, and you will."

Imagine how weak your mind becomes when you continue to put negative energy into your thoughts and words by making up excuses. If you look at yourself in the mirror and give thought to your life, you will realize there is no validity to your excuses, as they are simply concocted to take the easy way out, to linger in a life of mediocrity, and to persist in doubt and fear instead of taking the steps needed to walk in the light of success. Think about what you say and what you think, and you will realize these excuses are just that—excuses. Let's examine the latter part of the phrase "things got in the way."

You must be able to convince yourself the things that got in the way were more important and necessary to achieving your goals or not. If they were indeed more important, this is not an excuse but a validation of the choice you made toward a goal and achieved it. If they were not as important, then it is an excuse and one that no one could be proud of using. In life, we have choices to make each day. These choices are influenced by our attitudes, self-esteem or lack thereof, or our belief in ourselves as the greatest masterpiece on earth.

If we are positive in each of these, we become what we think about in our attitudes. Our life's goals are manifested in our efforts to achieve such goals, but first, we must have these attributes and set goals. Without goals, we only have excuses as to why things got in the way of achieving the goals we never set. I guarantee that if I ask 100 people what their goals are, less than half have no goals, forty-five or more will have goals but say other things got in the way of achieving those goals (I call those 'dreams' and not 'goals'), and the remaining five are doing what they need to do to go above and beyond their current day-to-day activities in pursuit of their goals and they are invariably achieving them.

3. Maybe I can, but…

This is likely one of the most tragic excuses of all. Not only does it have the word "but", which is almost always followed by an excuse, but it also has the phrase "Maybe I can". Whether you want to accept this fact or not, the word "maybe" is a negative term denoting a lack of confidence, which leaves everything to luck. Positive people don't say "maybe" or "I'll try"—they say, "I can," "I will," or "Consider it done."

These positive affirmations, which make up one's vocabulary and mindset, are seldom, if ever, followed by 'but'. They are driven by a desire to "do" and not to think, indefinitely, about whether it can be done. It is amazing how a positive attitude changes your perspective on everything you do.

It leads to a positive mindset, which leads to a "I can" mentality, and consequently results in positive results and the achievement of your goals. There will be challenges, as well as times when you go for the gold and fall short, but true success often happens after you fall short. Do you make excuses, give up, weep like a baby, and blame yourself or others for not achieving your goals, or do you persevere, remaining steadfast and committed to succeeding?

"Maybe I can, but…" is seldom the thinking of someone who believes in success and does what is required to achieve it. Instead, it is usually voiced by those who are fearful and doubtful about their own abilities and their capacity to do amazing things. It is the reason why many never realize their dreams and often use these words, not realizing the greatest impediment to their success is their thinking, which is manifested in their words and inaction.

You will see me reference mindset often, as the mind is indeed a terrible thing to waste. Imagine spending the same amount of time on negative thoughts and excuses compared to positive thoughts without excuses. The time it takes to think positive or negative thoughts is the same, so why would you want to waste time going nowhere in the pursuit of nothing, as negative leads to nowhere except into the doldrums of despair, misery, and mediocrity?

4. I had planned to do it, but...

Have you ever heard someone say these words? Have you ever said these words? I confess I did so on many occasions until I finally realized I was lying to myself all along.

In fact, most people who say these words never actually planned to do what they said, and even if they did, they have reasons ready for why they never got around to it. If anyone uses these words, they never really "planned'" at all or else they are supremely terrible planners who should consider adding the skills of "planning and doing" to their "to-do" list for areas of improvement.

However, the "to-do" list is likely also a farse which doesn't get done. Why? Creating a list of things to do, while important, does not end there. The items on the list must be mini goals, requiring a commitment "to do" them in the allotted period.

If not, they never get done and more excuses abound, such as "life just got in the way." Really? Then the list is meaningless, as is the one who creates a list and does not consider the presence of life's challenges and day-to-day activities. It is like having a list of what to take on a hike during the rainy season, which doesn't include an umbrella, and act surprised when it rains.

Essentially, they can't blame the rain, as such excuses have little to no validity. I challenge anyone to come up with a good reason why any of these excuses hold water for a long period of time.

Using the word "but" almost always comes with an excuse. Most of us do not even realize that we say "but" and use excuses so often to explain why we have not achieved what we ought to achieve in life. Many are clueless unless someone points it out, and then the "Oh Shit!!!" moment hits them in the face.

Many of us have these moments, but the majority 'come to Jesus' for a moment and then revert to unfulfilled lives, supported by comforting excuses that success and living a life of purpose are not in their DNA. Some of us believe our current life of struggling to make ends meet is the best we can do.

WRONG, WRONG, WRONG, as a person becomes what a person thinks, imagining the gift of the mind and thought is FREE.

The choice is indeed ours—to choose a more meaningful life if the one we are living is not what we want or believe we deserve. It is worth stating that some excuses are valid when made immediately following an event or non-event.

For example, "I had planned to write to you, but my father passed away suddenly." It is absolutely acceptable in the moment, but does it remain acceptable or valid if the passing of one's father occurred months ago or even over a year ago? My statement may seem insensitive; however, I dare say that making such a statement is an excuse.

A more truthful statement is, "I meant to write to you, but my father passed away and I forgot to write, as you were not on my mind and writing to you was not a priority."

Now, I know you would never say such words, even though it is likely the truth. Excuses are a way to sugarcoat the truth, while factual statements are not excuses but simply facts. Another example which I have heard many times can best be described in the following dialogue.

Me: Did you meet Mr. Rich last month?

John: I wanted to meet Mr. Rich when he was at our office, but I missed him.

Me: Ok, but his office is in the city, only three blocks away?

John: Yes, but he was here at our office and it was a great opportunity to meet him, and I missed the opportunity.

Me: Ok, I guess it was not that important after all.

John: It was important, as I have a proposal that I would like to present to him, but I missed him when he was at our office.

Me: Is there a problem with you walking over to his office, or calling to set up a meeting, or reaching out to someone in his office for an introduction?

John: I could, but he is probably busy, and I don't know anyone at his office. Do you know Mr. Rich or anyone at his office?

Does this dialogue sound familiar? Have you heard or experienced something similar? Have you been 'John' in the above dialogue? Now is the time to look deep within your soul and be honest with yourself. Why are you in your current life situation?

The answer to rising from the doldrums begins and ends with you. Can you see how tragic the above dialogue is? These kinds of excuses are driven by insecurity, fears, and doubts, which cripple the mind, so you do not think and therefore do not embrace the power from within.

Notice how John uses the word "but" in every response to my questions. Consider the simplicity of John just googling Mr. Rich and getting the needed information, or inquiring of others, then walking down to his office or calling his office to take the first step to achieving what he wants—presenting his proposal to Mr. Rich; even if he had to attempt doing so several times, as anything worth doing is worth persevering. This is not the 19th century, as information is readily available more than ever if we choose to look and have the burning desire to persevere and progress.

There is access to limitless information on the internet as well as access to people and resources on social media, so no one has a valid excuse for not pursuing any data they desire. Imagine that, apart from the invention of the internet, some of the greatest inventions and successes in the past 200 years were accomplished without technological advancements. Yet they occurred, and those who envisioned them were able to achieve what many felt was impossible. With today's technological advancements, what is your excuse? I dare say you have none. In the instance above, the worst that could have happened is that John might not get to see Mr. Rich, or Mr. Rich might say no to the proposal. However, is Mr. Rich the only individual to whom John could present his proposal?

I would make the bold assumption that the answer to the question is 'NO'. However, John's insecurity has led him to live a life void of critical thinking. He does not realize the power he has from within, nor does he trust he has skills and talents to offer as much, if not more, than anyone else. He lacks belief in himself.

People who want something badly enough do not complain about what they want or the challenging path to get it. They do not make excuses for not being able to get it. Instead, these individuals make the opportunities happen because when one is hungry and needs to be fed, nothing else matters.

If an able-bodied person is hungry enough, they will find food. The same is true for achieving your goals. If the goal is one you feel is crucial to your survival, you will accomplish it. However, if you have a safety net, you can always retreat to your comfort zone and continue making excuses as to why you have not and likely will not achieve your goals. If you take anything from this chapter, it should be the fact that you must avoid using the word 'but' followed by an excuse at all costs.

When you hear yourself using the word "but," correct yourself immediately. Over time, you will become a more positive and thoughtful person regarding your words, as your thinking drives your words, which ultimately drive your actions and your results.

I remember the United Negro College Fund (UNCF) commercials, in which Lou Rawls would say, "A mind is a terrible thing to waste." This quote is timeless, and I fully agree with it.

From this moment on, I urge you to use your mind wisely and consider what you say. Measure your thoughts and your words based on whether they are negative and full of excuses or positive and full of promise, conviction, courage, and nonconformity to those who remain in their own state of disrepair.

The choice is yours!

13

CONCLUSION

"In the quest to be a better version of yourself, if you know you are ignorant, yet do nothing about it, that is the greatest sin."

Your excuses have been debunked. As you read along, did you feel the pinch? Could you sense a push in the right direction? Was a fire ignited in your "belly" to follow your dreams? Did you awaken from an excuse-filled slumber encouraged that you now know your purpose and have all that it takes to pursue and fulfill your dreams?

If my taking this journey was not clear to you from reading this book, I am on this journey with you, too. I may be further along than some of you, and yet, in life, there are always more lessons to learn, so it is my wish that we can learn and succeed together.

If we stop learning, we stop living and just exist. The fact is, we don't need excuses. Each of us has one purpose and one purpose alone—to serve others. It is a challenge one we must meet head-on to fulfill.

We must discover our talents and skills, develop our philosophy of life, and utilize our gifts to live a life of purpose with meaning. Doing so is more a matter of harnessing the power within us than searching for our purpose.

It requires that we believe in ourselves. Within you is the power to say, "I can, and I will," and take the action needed without excuses. As I "penned my thoughts," I wanted to make it clear that you do not need a 12-step program or a specific list of things to do as advised by anyone, as your journey is an individual one and will be led in the right direction once the following is at the forefront of your consciousness.

1. Understand and accept that your purpose is to serve others—not simply for service's sake but doing so with meaning.

2. To do so with meaning, you must accept the fact that you have talents that need to be understood, harnessed, and nurtured. If you believe you do not have talents, you must find at least one, as we all were born with gifts. Not everyone has the same talents, but we absolutely have talents. This is imperative, as there is no way for you to live a life with meaning without using your talents.

3. Action - Knowing your purpose and accepting that you have talents are of no utility if you do not use the talents in pursuit of service to others. In addition to the above, the following prayer, widely known as the Serenity prayer, is essential to completing your understanding of the above.

"God grant me the serenity to accept the things I cannot change, courage to change the things I can, and

> ***the wisdom to know the difference***, *living one day at a time; enjoying one moment at a time; taking this world as it is and not as I would have it; trusting that You will make all things right if I surrender to Your will; so that I may be reasonably happy in this life and supremely happy with You forever in the next. Amen."*
>
> Reinhold Niebuhr

I thought it necessary to share this prayer, which I believe to be most impactful on my journey. However, I have highlighted the first section which is often used by many without completing the full prayer. Why is that? Well, everyone can relate to the section in bold, while not everyone believes in God, in the afterlife, or in a passive attitude toward life.

Remember, my philosophy is that if faith without works is dead, then one should go through life with an eagerness, excitement, and expectation that what they believe to be so can be if they have the faith, desire, and perseverance to pursue it. Let me share with you why there is no 12-step program to remove oneself from self-inflicted misery or imprisonment.

I believe the above part of the prayer in bold is the center of all that is necessary before one goes through the acknowledgment of knowing one's purpose, accepting one's talents, and using them to live a life of purpose with meaning.

To identify the difference between two or more things, one must have the wisdom to first know what these things are. However, in this case, there are only two things for one to consider: 1) things that one can change and 2) things that one cannot change. Understanding the difference is critical to the first part of the prayer, having the serenity to accept the things one cannot change. Now, once you have understood what you can and cannot change, the question is, "should you change the things you can, just because you can?"

I'll discuss this further below. Firstly, the things you cannot change should be easy to see, but one has to first believe they are masterpieces with a mind to do extraordinary things before one can make the assessment, as many fall into the trap of thinking they cannot change their circumstances, and therefore are left living a life of serenity in quiet desperation; not realizing that they accepted the things they could actually change, as things they cannot.

Never fall into this trap, as it is lethal to the core. Have you ever heard anyone say they cannot do something and are calm about it, as they have resolved to the fact they cannot, only to be challenged and have them realize they can? While this prayer is powerful, many miss this important point that serenity only comes from absolutely knowing one cannot change something. For example, I can't stop the sun from rising, I can't make someone love me, I can't fly as a human, BUT I can pull the shades down to avoid the sun from waking me up in the morning, I can love, I can build an airplane that flies, even if I can't fly in human form. You see, it is very important to never close your mind to the endless potential and possibilities that your mind can imagine, create, and aspire to do extraordinary things. The only things that one should find serenity in accepting are the things that one cannot possibly humanly do.

You will find that there are more things that the mind can aspire to achieve than not achieve. Secondly, in life, when you experience the little and big things, it is important to ask yourself, "if I can change these things, does it in any way benefit my pursuit of the purpose of serving others, using the talents I have?" If the answer is no, then there is no need to waste time with what I call the little things.

Family, friends, loved ones, and society may try to force you into the trap of wasting time on what does not matter to your purpose. You need to resist the urge to allow them to bring you down into the depths of despair, gossip, and insignificant undertakings that have no validity and usefulness, or alignment with your purpose.

Have you ever had conversations with family or friends, discussing what someone did or did not do, and found it trivial? Why should you care that your uncle wore different-colored socks? It is fine to make the observation, but it is not worth making it a mortal sin or spending what may seem like hours in conversation about such trivialities. Your aunt seems to have not finished her make-up in the way you think she should, so what?

Has your life changed significantly? Has someone fallen sick or died as a result, and more importantly, how have you helped your aunt, if she even needs or wants your help? Is any of this meaningful talk?

Some call it small talk, but would it not be great to have conversations about the joy of finding solutions to problems that help people using your talents, rather than waste time in hypocritical talks that you would otherwise not have with the person themselves? Don't misunderstand me here, as it is also such joy just fooling around and having fun with the ones who uplift you in every way.

Surely, it beats useless talk and unnecessary judgments about others. The point here is that just because you can change something, doesn't mean should you do so unless it has meaning in fulfilling your purpose.

Therefore, anytime an issue comes up, and you have determined that you can change it, consider going through the assessment of whether changing it is aligned with your purpose. This is what is needed so you can have courage amidst the noise of those who may attempt to influence your decisions. In short, the courage you seek should be used on the things that you can change that make a positive difference in your life and the life of others.

The key here is that once you realize the significance in alignment with your purpose of being able to change the things you can, you must have the courage to do so.

Many lack the courage and thus use excuses to keep them from making a difference and using their talents to live a life of purpose with meaning. When you understand you are here to serve your fellow human beings, then how to accomplish it should be a self-fulfilling prophecy, and yet it often is not.

Why? We get caught up in the hustle and bustle of living and fall into our pattern of excuses. Instead, we need to pursue our purpose—using our gifts to serve others. In "No More Excuses," one of my goals was to help you recognize the excuses most of us use daily without even realizing it. Excuses do nothing more than result in you avoiding the next step in your life. Excuses hold you back from living a life of purpose with meaning.

Once you know how excuses work, you have the power to stop using them and instead set your mind to believe in yourself and walk forward successfully in your purpose. The greatest power in the universe is your mind; all you need to do is learn to use it, putting away excuses that exist as poison to your soul and are toxic to your purpose. Now you know, and, I dare to say, are "spiritually awakened" in your newfound knowledge.

You have the opportunity to take the first steps toward living your life of purpose with meaning—a fulfilled life. How do you do it? Begin by serving others in your own unique way, shape, or form. Do not allow yourself to be pushed in the wrong direction by the work you may find yourself stuck in or by society, which seems to want everyone to follow its norms and conform.

CONCLUSION

By no means should you ever conform or use excuses to join the crowd of the many who are imprisoned by their own excuses. Be bold and take the road less traveled and enjoy the journey of self-discovery now that you know your purpose, you have embraced your skills and will use them to live a life filled with passion, fulfillment, and meaning.

Finally, it is important for me to reiterate that this book is not meant to be religious, as it is based on a spiritual awakening that focuses on the power within us all, whether we believe in God or not, as God and the greatness therein is and will always be up to you, not persons of the flesh to define.

The present moment can be your time to take the first steps on your journey to finding meaning and fulfillment in your life as you pursue your purpose with no more excuses!

The choice is yours!

ABOUT THE AUTHOR

Lincoln E.C. Greenidge is an award-winning finance professional with over 25 years of public company experience in finance and operations, spanning five continents. He is not a philosopher, a clinical psychologist, or a social worker. He is just an everyday person seeking to do extraordinary things by inspiring others to find meaning in their lives by using their skills and talents to pursue actions that enhance their joy and fulfill their purpose. Most of his inspiration comes to him while walking his dog, Rocky, at his home in White Sulphur Springs, Montana.

www.ingramcontent.com/pod-product-compliance
Lightning Source LLC
Chambersburg PA
CBHW041204150726
48006CB00016B/2111